Sewing for Dolls

Sherralyn St. Clair

COPYRIGHT

ACKNOWLEGEMENTS

Front cover: The brunette doll is Emma from Springfield® Collection. Springfield® Collection dolls can be purchased in craft stores in the US, Canada, and Europe. They can also be ordered on line.

ABOUT THE FRONT COVER

You can find a free pattern for Kitty's stuffed cat at www.sherralynsdolls.com. Select Florabunda's page from the buttons at the top of the main page. On Florabunda's page select beginning sew projects from that page's directory. The pattern for Kitty's doll, Twinkle, is found in the companion book, *Sewing for Mini Dolls* or for purchase and download at www.sherralynsdolls.com.

INTRODUCTION

This book contains patterns for 18" (46 cm) doll clothing. I have tried the clothing on American Girl® dolls, dolls from the Springfield® Collection, and other similar dolls. Because I have received several requests for shoe patterns, the book includes patterns for sneakers, bedroom slippers, and Mary Jane shoes. If you would like to make your own doll instead of purchasing a doll, I have added a pattern for Kitty, an (18" 46 cm) cloth doll. Kitty can be made with optional details such as fingers, toes, and ears.

If you would like to make the mini doll Kitty is holding on the cover, the pattern is in the companion book, *Sewing for Mini Dolls*. That book includes a pattern for Twinkle, a 6½" (16.5 cm) doll and clothing that fits her and other mini dolls, such as American Girl® Mini. Twinkle's pattern is also available at www.sherralynsdolls.com.

At the beginning of each project I list the supplies and equipment that you will need to make the doll or garment. I also list the skills that are explained in the instructions. Sometimes you are referred to the book's appendix called **Tools, Tips, and Techniques**. I discuss equipment and sewing techniques in this appendix. If you would like a copy of **Tools, Tips, and Techniques** with *color* illustrations you can download it free from the pattern page of my website, www.sherralynsdolls.com.

After each set of instructions are full size patterns for 18" (46 cm) doll clothing or for Kitty, the cloth doll. The pattern pieces are labeled with the name of the doll part or clothing item. Copy or trace the patterns and use them in constructing your projects.

If you are using a copier, you want the patterns printed full size. Before cutting out your pattern pieces from fabric, check the copied patterns against the patterns in the book to verify that they are the correct size and adjust your copier setting if necessary.

I invite you to visit www.sherralynsdolls.com for sewing tips, ideas for doll accessories, free patterns, and free children's stories. If you want to see color pictures of dolls wearing clothing from this book, check the Pattern Page or the Book Page.

Email me at sherralyn@www.sherralynsdolls.com if you have questions, suggestions, or just want to chat about dollmaking.

Here are the symbols found on the patterns and in the instructions of this book:

- Indicates the pattern pieces for 18" (46 cm) doll clothing or for the Kitty doll.
- **Tips** p (page number) refers you to the page in the appendix, **Tools, Tips, and Techniques,** that contains additional information about the sewing project.
- _ _ _ indicates the stitch line.
- · · − · · indicates stay-stitching.
- ·········· indicates top stitching.
- ‖‖‖‖‖‖‖‖ indicates where to gather the fabric.
- · · _ _ _ indicates where to align the pockets on the garment and the sneaker shoe sides on the tongue/toe.
- · · · · · indicates where to fold a fabric piece after it has been cut.
- · · _ _ _ indicates stencil placement.
- ⸻✂⸻ indicates the location of clips.
- indicates the right side of the fabric.

CONTENTS

This pattern includes the doll itself as well as panties, a camisole, and sandals. If you have some previous sewing experience and enjoy sewing, this doll will be fun to sew. The pattern includes optional details like fingers, toes, and ears. As an option there are instructions explaining how to prepare and print a fabric sheet with faces.

Your doll will be cozy and huggable in this this cotton flannel nightgown and fleece sleep cap. Your doll can choose her favorite from six animal slipper patterns: bunny, cat, dog, mouse, pig, or bear.

This pattern is a fairly simple, basic pattern. It is a fast and easy to make and can be embellished in many ways.

Make your doll a T-shirt and then add long pants, shorts, or an A-line skirt. Add the optional pocket to the pants or skirt to make jeans or khakis. Finish dressing your doll with socks and a stylish pair of sneakers.

Your doll can dance her princess slippers to pieces while wearing her ballgown and crown. On less formal occasions, when she is not being a princess, she can wear her classic dress with her Mary Jane shoes.

This appendix provides additional details for some of the sewing techniques and procedures used in the patterns.

Kitty Doll

- About 8 oz (220 g) of polyester stuffing
- Two 30 mm doll joints and two 35 mm doll joints
- Seam sealant and wax paper
- Fabric glue stick
- For printing the face onto fabric (optional)
  - Freezer paper, Sulky Sticky+®, or quilt basting spray
  - Masking tape
- For coloring the face
  - Boxes of waterproof colored pencils in primary colors and earth tones
  - Thin line permanent markers in red, black, brown, and blue or brown for the eyes.
  - White acrylic paint and a thin brush
  - Powdered blush (optional)
- For yarn wig
  - 1 skein of yarn for hair in the color of your choice
  - Matching thread
  - Permanent fabric glue
  - Narrow masking tape for construction
- Size 14 commercial wig rather than yarn, if you prefer
- For clothing
  - 7" (18 cm) of cotton fabric (pants and camisole)
  - ⅛" (3 mm) wide elastic (pants)
  - ¼" (6 mm) wide lace edging (pants and camisole)
  - Ribbon (camisole and sandals)
  - Small applique (optional for camisole)
  - Hook and loop tape (camisole)
  - Stiff felt (sandals)
  - Decorative buttons or small appliques (optional for sandals)
  - Tacky Glue® (sandals)

Equipment

- Basic sewing tools (**Tips** p. 84)
- An open embroidery foot to use when following sewing lines for arms and legs
- One 2" (5 cm) needle for sculpting toes
- Stuffing tools such as: a hemostat, a chopstick, and an inexpensive paintbrush (use the smooth end)
- Cardboard for wrapping hair yarn
- A bodkin for threading elastic through the casing (pants)
- Clothes pins (use as clamps when gluing sandals)

Supplies

- ½ yd (46 cm) 100% cotton fabric in skin color of your choice
- Thread for sewing doll in slightly lighter color than fabric
- Prismacolor® peach pencil or other washable pencil and thin line air soluble pen for marking

Introduction

These instructions describe the construction of an 18" (46 cm) Kitty cloth doll and her camisole, pants, and sandals.

Preparing the Fabric and Cutting the Pattern Pieces

Not all the pattern pieces for Kitty are simply pinned to the fabric and then cut out.

The face is traced or printed on fabric.

The arms, legs, and ears are traced templates. These parts are then sewn before they are cut out.

The head-sides and backs and the body-fronts and body-backs are cut and marked like traditional pattern pieces.

If you are printing the face on fabric, I think that it is best to begin with the face, because you will use a printing paper size piece of fabric. It is easier to arrange your pattern pieces on the fabric if this piece is removed from your fabric first.

The Face

You may either trace the face of the doll onto fabric by hand or, you may print the Face Page included with the patterns directly onto a piece of cotton fabric using an ink jet copier/printer.

Three Methods for Tracing the Face

- Hold the pattern and fabric up to a window to trace markings. This method is easier if the pattern and fabric are held to the window with drafting tape. (I think masking tape is too strong.)
- A clear plastic box picture frame works fairly well when tracing pattern markings. It should be propped up at an angle rather than resting flat on a table. Another solution is to have a battery powered light under the plastic box. The light should be behind the pattern that you are tracing.
- My favorite tracing method is a light box or table. I bought a small inexpensive one years ago. Larger ones may be fairly pricey. I use a small amount of drafting tape to hold the pattern and fabric to my light box.

Printing the face on Fabric

To print the doll face on cloth, you should have an ink jet copier/printer. I think that it is easier to make a paper copy of the face page rather than copying directly from the book to fabric.

- Cut a sheet of freezer paper 8½" by 11".
  - I have found that Reynold's® brand freezer paper works better than house brands.
  - I have also used Sulky® Sticky+ stabilizer paper in lieu of the freezer paper. This comes in rolls and sheets. The rolls are slightly narrower than 8½" but are wide enough for this use.
  - Another alternative I have tried is to spray a piece of 8½" by 11" (letter size) paper with quilt basting spray.
  - The patterns are narrow enough that you should be able to use A4 paper if that is more conveniently available than letter size paper. However, I have not tried this myself.
- Cut a piece of cotton doll making fabric that is slightly larger than the prepared freezer paper.
- The straight of grain should run down the length of the fabric. Note the straight of grain arrow on the Face Page.
- Make sure that the fabric is cut straight and is pressed flat.
- Lay the waxy side of the freezer paper on the wrong side of the fabric. In other methods the sticky side of the paper goes to the wronger side of the fabric. The 11" side of the paper should be lined up with the straight of grain. A small amount of fabric should show all around the paper.
- Iron the backing sheet to the fabric. Use the cotton setting of your iron. Press down on the fabric while you are ironing. Try to iron out all the air bubbles. Make sure that the fabric is stuck to the backing, especially at edges and corners.

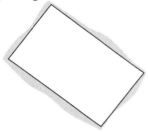

- Trim the fabric to the size of the paper.
- This step is optional. To help the prepared sheet pass smoothly through the printer, I like to fold a strip of masking tape across the end of the sheet that will feed into the printer first. Fold the tape so that one half of the tape width is on the fabric side of the sheet and the other half of the tape width is on the paper side of the sheet. If you use tape, make sure that the tape is very flat and smooth. Do not leave creases or air pockets. After I smooth out the tape, I sometimes cover it with a pressing cloth and iron it.

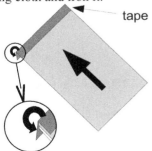

tape

Printing the Face

- Place the prepared sheet in you copier so that the faces will be printed on the fabric side of the sheet.
- Choose the Face Page with gray outline features for a light skin doll and the Face Page with black outline features for a darker skin doll.
- Each Face Page also has a face for my Florabunda and Twinkle dolls. If you have a pattern, you can make either a Florabunda or a Twinkle doll with the fabric scraps from Kitty. Otherwise, use the extra faces for practice coloring the face.
- Copy the Face Page.
- Peel the tape and backing paper away from the fabric.
- Sometimes the paper backing can be used two or more times.

Completing the Face

- Use waterproof pens and pencils. Follow the directions: "Coloring the Face" below. I have found that it is better to give faces printed in black ink black eye brows and lashes. Faces printed with gray ink can have black or brown brows and lashes.

Coloring the Face

1. Use your printed on fabric face outline or the traced face outline.
2. Color over brows and the top arch of the eye with brown or black pen. Fill in irises with blue or brown pencil. Outline irises with blue or brown pen to match pencil color. Fill in pupils with black pen. I have also made a green-eyed face by coloring the iris with green pencil and outlining the iris rim with green pen. Paint the whites of the eyes and eye reflections with white acrylic paint. The pattern does not indicate the reflection dots' positions. The following figure gives a suggestion for placement of a reflection dot, but you may place them wherever you choose. Add nostril dots with brown pen. Outline nose shadows with orange pencil. Fill in lips with red pencil. Outline lips and lip part with red pen.

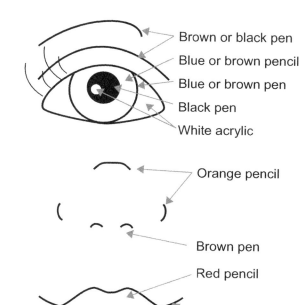

Brown or black pen
Blue or brown pencil
Blue or brown pen
Black pen
White acrylic

Orange pencil

Brown pen

Red pencil

Red pen

Marking and Sewing Arms, Legs, and Ears

1. Cut out the arm, leg, and ear templates from the copied pattern page containing the templates. Using a peach pencil or air soluble pen trace two arms, two legs, and two ears on wrong side of a folded piece of your fabric. Mark the spaces to be left open. The peach pencil works on both light and dark fabric.
2. If you have freezer paper, you can trace your templates onto a piece of freezer paper. Cut out the tracings and iron the waxy side of the tracing onto your fabric instead of drawing the pieces on the fabric. Use a relatively cool iron setting such as one for polyester or for cotton blends. As you can see from the photo below, there is plenty of room for arm and leg templates for Florabunda or Twinkle, if you decide to make a small doll also.

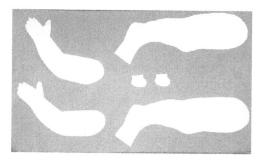

3. Use an open embroidery foot to sew on traced lines or next to the freezer paper. I like to place my Ott-lite® on my machine table to my left to help me see the lines. If you have a needle-down option on your machine, it is helpful for this type of sewing. Do not sew on areas of templates marked leave open, including the toe space on the foot.
4. Set the sewn pieces aside while you cut and mark the head and body.

Cutting and Marking the Head and Body

1. Cut out two head-sides and two head-backs. Mark the darts and ear placement lines on the wrong side of the head-sides. Mark the chin dart on the wrong side of the face. Mark the notches. (**Tips** p.88) Don't forget Florabunda or Twinkle's head-back and body-fronts and body-backs, if you are also making a small doll.
2. Cut out body-fronts and body-backs.
3. Mark dots to show the joint openings for arms and legs on the body-fronts and body-backs. Mark the A and B dots on the body center-back. Mark the notches.

Head and Body

Making the Ears

Ears are optional and are attached when you sew the head-side darts. The head-side darts must be sewn with or without ears.

1. Cut out the two ears that you have sewn using the ear template. Leave a ⅛" (3 mm) seam allowance.

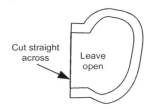

2. Turn the ears right side out.
3. Trace the top stitching line on each ear with air soluble pen.
4. Put a very small amount of polyester stuffing in each ear.

5. Machine stitch the marked top stitching line on each ear.

Making the Head

1. Follow steps a), b), and c) if you are making ears. If you are not making ears, go to step 2.
   a) Cut the ear slits on each head-side piece. I like to start the slit with a seam ripper and then cut the slit with embroidery scissors.

b) On the right side of each head-side, slip the raw edge of the ear into the ear slit. Make sure that the ears are positioned correctly.
c) Fold the darts on each side of the head. Keep raw edges of the ears even with the ear slit in each dart. Starting at the raw edge of each ear, ¼" (6 mm) of each ear should be caught in the dart seam.

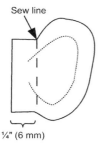

2. Pin and sew the head-side darts.

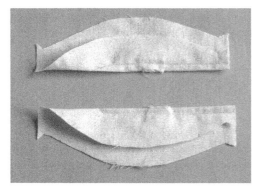

3. Press the head-side darts and check to see if the ears are placed correctly.

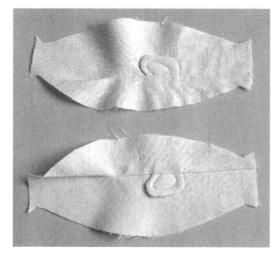

4. Sew the chin dart on the face.
5. Right sides together pin, the head-sides to the face matching the single and double notches. Machine stitch. Trim the seam to ⅛" (3 mm). Starting at the raw edge, cut the chin dart open ½" (12 mm) on the dart fold line. Steam press the seams toward the head-side on both sides of the face and press the first ½"

(12 mm) of the dart seam flat. If you did not use waterproof pens and pencils on the face, finger press the seams and the dart.

6. Right sides together, match the triple notches and sew the head-backs to the head-sides.

7. Stay-stitch the top of the head ¼" (6 mm) from the raw edge, as indicated on the pattern pieces.
8. Set the head aside. Do not sew the head-backs together until after the head has been attached to the body.

Making Body-Front and Body-Back

1. With right sides together, match the double notches. Sew body-front down the center-front line using a ¼" (6 mm) seam. (I like to back stitch all the neck seams.)

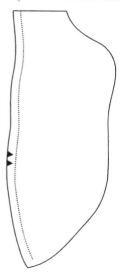

2. Finger press the seams open.

3. With right sides together, sew body-backs together down the center-back beginning at point A on the lower part of the back.

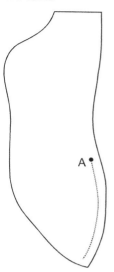

4. Do not sew from the neck to point B at this time.
5. Finger press the seams.

Assembling Body

1. With right sides together, pin the body-front to the body-back. Match the single notches and the joint-opening dots.
2. Sew all the way around the body using a ¼" (6 mm) seam. Leave the joint placement areas open. Do not sew from center-back neck to point B until the head has been attached to the body.

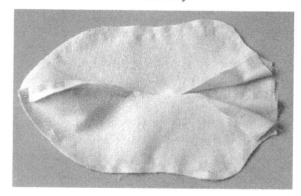

Aligning Head and Body

Begin with the body wrong side out. The back of the body is visible. The head is also wrong side out. The raw edges of the chin dart seam are visible. The top of the head with the stay-stitching will go into the body opening first. The chin dart will go in last.

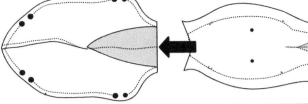

Push the head into the body cavity.

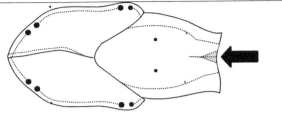

Align the raw edges of the base of the head and the raw edges of the body neck. Pin the head in place.
The right sides of the head and body fabrics are touching. The raw edges of the base of the head and body neck are even. The chin dart seam and the body center-front seam are matched.

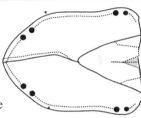

Attaching Head and Body

1. First match the base of the head to the body neck. Follow the diagrams above to align the two pieces correctly.
2. To place the head on the body correctly, pin the head to the body before sewing them together. Start by pinning the center-front seam to the chin dart seam. From this point pin the head to the body in one direction. Stop when one side of the head center-back is pinned to the body center-back. Return to the center-front and pin the pieces together in the other direction.
3. Baste and then machine stitch the head to the body.
4. Pull the head out of the body. Keep the head/body unit wrong side out.

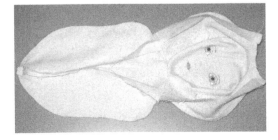

Sewing the Head and Body Center-Back and Stuffing the Head

1. Match and pin the four notches on the head center-back. Match and pin the neck seams. Last, match and pin the B dots on the body center-back.

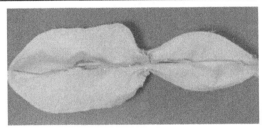

2. Start sewing at the top of the head above the stay-stitching and stop at the B dots on the body center-back.
3. Turn the head and body right side out through the stuffing opening.
4. Turn the fabric under at the stay-stitching at the top of the head. Gather this fabric by hand-stitching. Secure the thread and sew around the stitching a second time for strength. When you have finished, the gathered circle should be about ⅝" (1.5 cm) in diameter.

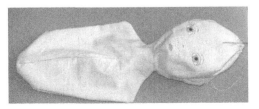

5. Stuff the head firmly through the stuffing opening in the body's center-back.
6. Set the head/body aside while you work on the arms and legs. The body cannot be stuffed until you add the arms and legs.

Arms and Legs

Cutting out the Legs

Cut out the sewn legs. Leave a ⅛" (3 mm) allowance in most areas. Leave a ¼" (6 mm) allowance around stuffing openings. Leave a ¼" (6 mm) allowance at the top and bottom of the foot. The larger seam allowance makes it easier to match the foot seams.

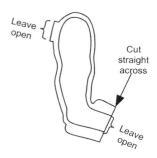

Sewing the Foot

1. Finger press the seams of the top and bottom of the foot open. Bring the top and bottom of each foot together. Match the seams carefully. I like to use a touch of sewing glue stick to keep the matched seams together.

2. Cut out the foot and toe templates from the pattern page containing all the templates. Line up the sides of the foot template with the sides of the foot. The edge of the template should align with the edge of the toe opening. Line up the glued-together seams in the middle of the foot with the center line on the template. Trace the foot stitch line on the first foot with a fine tipped air soluble pen. Make sure that the line you draw touches the edge on each side of the foot.

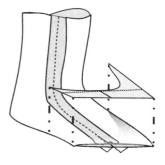

3. Flip the template to trace a mirror image on the second foot so that you will have a right and left foot.

4. Sew each foot seam on the line you have drawn from the template. Trim the foot seams to an ⅛" (3 mm) seam. Turn the legs right side out through the stuffing opening. Stuff the feet firmly. Continue stuffing each foot until the stuffing is a little higher than the ankles, then sculpt the toes.

Marking the Toes

1. Push a pin through the toe template at each dot to make a small hole at the beginning of the line between each toe. Make tiny clips on the edge of the Toe Template at the end of each toe line. Lay the template on the top of the foot. Mark a dot through the hole at each beginning point with the air soluble pen. Mark a dot at each clip on the template edge. Remove the template. Connect the dots to draw a line between each toe that matches the same line on the template. The big toe and the second toe should be on one side of the leg/foot seam, the third, fourth, and fifth toes should be on the other side of the seam. The line between the second and third toes should be on the seam itself.

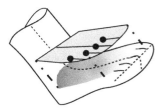

2. Place the template on the sole of the foot. Line up and mark the toe lines on the sole.

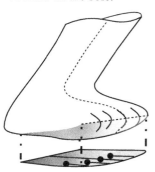

3. Mark the toe lines on the second foot. Be sure to place the template correctly so that you have a left and right foot.

Sculpting the toes

1. First you will round the corners on each side of the foot seam and then you will sculpt the toes.

2. Thread a needle and tie a small knot at one end. Push the needle into the foot/leg seam on the sole of the foot at square 1 as shown in the following figure. Bring the needle out at corner A. Pull the thread all the way through the foot and gently tug until the knot is inside the foot at square 1. Take a small stitch at corner A and send the needle back to the sole at square 1. The white dotted line in the figure indicates the thread when it is inside the foot. Pull gently on the thread until corner A is rounded. Take a small stitch at square 1 to secure the seam. Round corner B in the same manner, by taking a small stitch at corner B and returning to square 1. The black line shows the visible thread outside the foot. The black loop indicates the stitch at corner B before the thread has been pulled in. When you are satisfied with rounded corner B, secure the thread with one or two tiny stitches at square 1. Do not cut the thread. You will use the remaining thread to sculpt the toes. Add a little stuffing at the rounded corners to smooth the foot seam.

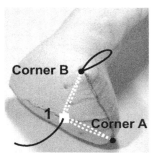

3. The dots in the figure below show the points you will use to sculpt the toes. Insert the needle back into square 1. Bring the needle out at dot 2 where the big toe starts. Wrap the thread around the edge of the foot to define the big toe by inserting the needle into point 3 on the sole of the foot. Push the needle back to dot 2 at the top of the foot. Gently pull the thread until you are satisfied with the shape of the big toe.

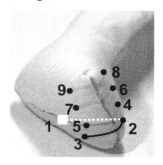

4. Put the needle back into dot 3 and bring it out through dot 4 as shown in the figure below. Loop the needle down to dot 5 and back to dot 4. Then shape this toe in the same way that you shaped the big toe.

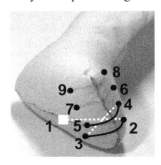

5. Continue down the foot until you have sculpted all the toes. Sometimes I take a tiny stitch on the seam line between dots 8 and 9 to make the line between toe four and the little toe lie correctly. After you have sculpted the little toe, take several tiny stitches in the sole at the point 9 to secure the thread. To hide the thread, bring the needle out through the sole at square 1. Pull the thread tightly before cutting it close to the fabric. When the thread is released, the end of the thread will go back inside the foot and be hidden.

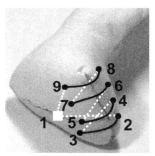

Adding Toenails

Toenails are optional. If you would like to add toenails, I suggest that you use your purple air soluble pen to lightly draw toenails on the toes. If you are not satisfied with the result, the ink will evaporate and you can try again. For unpainted nails go over the purple lines lightly with a waterproof brown pen. For polished nails, fill in the nails with acrylic paint or waterproof pen.

Continuing to Stuff the Legs

Continue stuffing the legs until the stuffing reaches the stuffing opening.

Cutting out the Arms

1. Cut out the sewn arms. Leave a ⅛" (3 mm) allowance in most areas. Leave a ¼" (6 mm) allowance around stuffing openings. Trim more closely around the hand and thumb. Clip all the spots where turning will stress

the seam. A pair of small sharp scissors helps to trim and clip accurately.

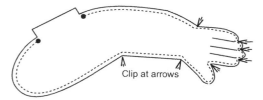

Clip at arrows

2. Use a seam sealant around the closely trimmed areas. Squeeze a few drops of sealant onto a sheet of waxed paper, dip a toothpick into the drops, and carefully go around the trimmed areas. Use the sealant sparingly.
3. As soon as you have applied the sealant, turn the arm right side out with a hemostat. Use a stuffing tool such as the non-bristle end of a small paint brush to turn the thumb and finger tips. Be patient and use slow, firm pressure when turning the thumb and fingertips. It is easy to push through a seam, if you use too much pressure.

Marking the Finger Lines

1. Push a pin through the template at the bottom of each finger line to make a small hole.
2. Lay the template on the hand. Mark a dot through the hole at the bottom of each finger line with a thin line air soluble pen. Remove the template.
3. Draw a line between each finger with air soluble pen. Start at the space between each fingertip and go to the dot at the bottom of each finger line.

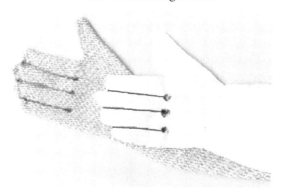

Sewing the Fingers

1. Pull enough starting thread from the spool and bobbin to use in threading a needle. Use needle- down if you have it on your machine.
2. Start at the bottom of each finger line where you marked the dot and sew on the line to the tip. Pivot the hand and sew on top of the first stitches back down to the bottom of the finger line.
3. Pull enough ending thread from the spool and bobbin to use in threading a needle. You will hide the ends of the threads after the hand and arm have been stuffed.

Stuffing the Fingers

1. Stuff each finger and the thumb firmly. Use small pieces of stuffing. Roll each wisp of stuffing between your finger and thumb until you have a small tight piece of stuffing about a third to half the length of the finger. Push each piece as far up the finger as you can before adding the next piece. Check to see if each finger is firmly stuffed before stuffing the palm.
2. Cut one or two pieces of quilt batting to roughly the size of the hand palm. If you do not have batting, you can try using three or four pieces of white flannel. Stuff palm/back of hand with quilt batting or flannel rather than fiberfill to keep the hand fairly flat. The quilt batting or flannel is optional. You can use fiberfill, but I am happier with my doll's hands when I use quilt batting. This photo illustrates the size and amount of stuffing for the fingers and palm/back of the hand.

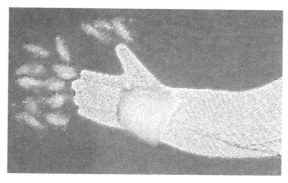

3. While stuffing the wrist, pinch the palm to keep the hand from being overly stuffed. Use large pieces of polyester fiberfill and do not allow the stuffing to flow into the hand.
4. Continue stuffing the arms until the stuffing reaches the stuffing opening.

Hiding the Finger Threads

1. Start on the palm of the hand. Use a needle threader to thread the two threads at the bottom of the first finger line. Insert the needle into the hand at the bottom of the last stitch. Do not go through the hand. Bring the needle out through the palm. Pull the thread tightly before cutting and clip the thread close to the fabric. When the thread is released, the end of the thread will go back inside the hand and be hidden. Hide all the finger threads on the palm side of the hand.

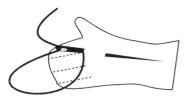

2. Turn the hand over and hide the three pairs of finger threads on the back of the hand.

Adding Fingernails

If you would like to add fingernails, follow the same directions as those for adding toenails.

Positioning the Arms and Legs

1. Lay the head/body unit on a table.
2. Lay the arms and legs on the table so that the parts of the arms and legs that will be touching the body are facing up. The thumbs should be pointing toward the head. The toes should be pointing away from the body. The little toes should be touching the table and the big toes should be visible. Transfer the Xs from the arm and leg templates to the sides of the arms and legs that are visible and will touch the doll's body.

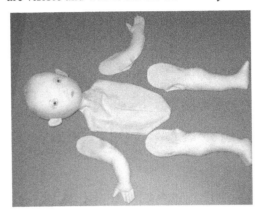

Attaching the Arms and Legs

1. Snip each marked X.
2. Apply a small amount of seam sealant.
3. Insert a 30 mm doll joint into each arm and a 35 mm doll joint into each leg through the snipped X.
4. Allow the seam sealant to dry.
5. Work through the stuffing opening while attaching all four joints.
6. Push the end of each arm joint into the body through the joint openings below the shoulder.
7. The inside of the arm should be touching the doll body.
8. Check the position of the hands before securing each joint.

9. Place a washer on the joint inside the body and then secure the arm to the body with the lock washer.

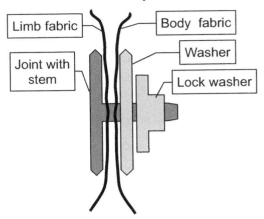

10. Push each of the leg joints into the body through the joint openings at the hips.
11. Secure the leg joints as you did the arm joints.
12. Finish stuffing the arms and legs. Then close the arms and legs with overcasting or the ladder stitch. (**Tips** p. 86)

Finishing Stuffing

1. Stuff the body firmly
2. Close the stuffing opening with the overcasting stitch.

Hair

You can use a size 14 commercial wig rather than making yarn hair, if you wish. If you prefer a yarn wig for your doll, use the following instructions to add hair to your doll.

Marking Cardboard for Yarn Wrapping

1. Use a 12" x 9"(30 cm x 23 cm) Piece of cardboard for the hair sides and center part. (I used the cardboard that Amazon uses to package its books for shipping.)
2. Mark a 5½" (14 cm) section on one short side of the board and label it "Side-Hair."

3. Mark a 7" (18 cm) section on the parallel side of the board and label it "Hair-Part"

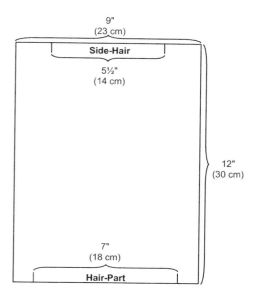

Wrapping and Machine Sewing the Side-Hair Yarn

1. Wrap the yarn around the length of the cardboard, between the lines you have marked "Side-Hair." You should have a section of yarn 12" x 5½" (30 cm x 14 cm).

2. Wrap narrow masking tape around the cardboard ½" (12 mm) from one side of loops. The small piece of tape in the photo was used to hold the yarn steady when I began wrapping it.

3. Do not cut the loops of yarn that are ½" (12 mm) from the tape. Carefully cut the loops on the opposite side of the cardboard.

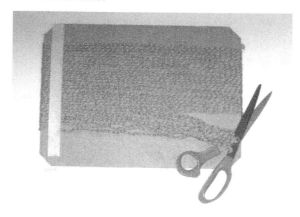

4. Remove the yarn from the board and rejoin the tape so that you still have a tape ½" (12 mm) from the looped yarn.

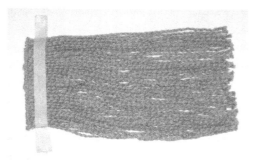

5. Sew the yarn on your machine with matching thread. Sew a ¼" seam from the loop side of the yarn. Remove the tape.

6. Wrap and sew another side-hair piece exactly as you made the first side-hair piece.

Attaching Two Side-Hair Pieces to the Doll's Head

1. Draw the hair line for the side-hair on the doll's head with an air soluble pen. Start on one head-side on the seam between the face and head-side. The line should be about even with the eyebrow. (The line's beginning point is shown as point A on the following figure.) The beginning of the hair line will be covered by the bangs when they are added.
2. The line should go behind the ear (point B) down the head-side and across the back. Stop at the center-back head seam (point C). The ending point C is not shown, but is indicated by the arrow.

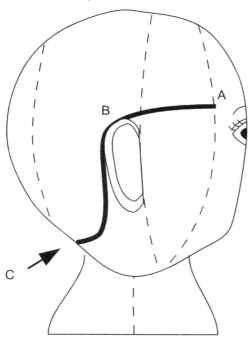

3. Draw the side-hair line on the other side of the head.
4. Make sure that the two lines look even.

5. Pin the yarn hair to each side of the head. Pin on the yarn's machine stitching below the yarn loops.

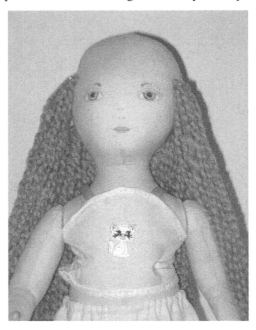

6. The two yarn side pieces should meet at the center-back of the doll's head. The yarn side-hair may be wider than the line from the eyebrow to the head center-back. If it is wider, fold it at both ends of the yarn section and re-pin it.

7. Hand sew the yarn to the doll's head on top of the machine stitching.

Wrapping and Machine Sewing the Bangs

1. Use a 6" x 6" (15 cm x 15 cm) piece of cardboard to wrap the bangs.

2. Mark a 5" (13 cm) section as shown.

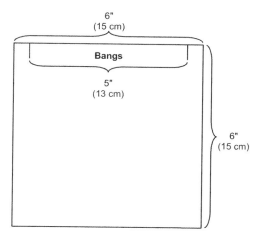

3. Wrap yarn around the bangs cardboard between the lines that you have drawn.
4. Wrap narrow masking tape around the cardboard 2" (5 cm) from one side of loops.

5. Do not cut the loops of yarn that are 2" (5 cm) from the tape at this time. Carefully cut the loops on the opposite side of the cardboard.

6. Remove the yarn from the board and rejoin the tape so that you still have a tape 2" (5 cm) from the looped yarn.

7. Sew 2" (5 cm) from the loop side of the yarn. Sew next to the tape without catching it with your machine needle. Remove the tape.

Attaching the Bangs to the Head

1. Pin the bangs to the forehead. Place the pins on the machine stitching line.
2. The bangs yarn should cover the forehead above the eyebrows. It should just cover the side-hair yarn where it touches the seam between the head-side and face.

3. The yarn behind the bangs should cover the top of the head including the hole surrounded by gathering stitches. This back hair will be covered by the yarn that will be parted to make braids.

4. Hand sew the bangs to the head on top of the machine stitching line.
5. Use fabric glue to hold the yarn behind the bangs to the top and back of the head. Leave the bangs yarn loose.
6. Carefully trim any yarn behind the bangs that does not lie neatly.

Wrapping and Machine Sewing the Part

1. Wrap the yarn around the length of the larger cardboard, between the lines you have marked "Hair-

Part." You should have a section of yarn 12" x 7" (30 cm x 18 cm).

2. Wrap narrow masking tape around the cardboard ¼" (6 mm) from one side of loops.
3. Carefully cut the loops on the opposite side of the cardboard from the tape.
4. Open out this section of yarn so that there is an area of yarn between two strips of tape.

5. Sew between the two strips of tape so that there is about 12" (30 cm) of yarn on each side of the machine stitching.

Attaching the Hair-Part to the Head

1. Arrange the yarn so that it starts at the bangs seam and the machine stitching runs down the middle of the head.

a) Your can pull the yarn above the ears and make a ponytail on each side of the head.

2. Pin in place. Use matching thread to sew the part in place along the machine stitching line.

b) You can leave the hair as ponytails or braid each ponytail.

c) You can also pull the yarn hair to the back of the head behind the ears and braid it.

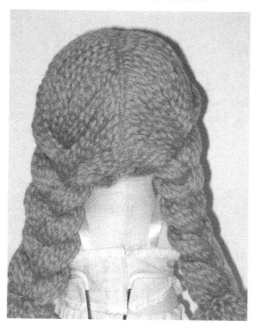

d) If you prefer, you can make French braids.

Finishing the Hair Style

1. Pull the side-hair yarn back and away from the face, so that the hand stitching and yarn loops are hidden.
2. The arrangement of yarn gives you several options for hair styles.

1. Cut the loops on the doll's bangs. Carefully trim the bangs if needed.

If you would like pink cheeks on your doll, add powdered blush on the finished doll. Put a small amount of blush on each cheek with a small brush or cotton swab. Rub the color in with a makeup sponge or dry washcloth.

Camisole

1. Cut out camisole. Mark the A and B dots on the wrong side of the fabric.
2. Sew lace around the top of the camisole.
   a) Lay the right side of the lace on the wrong side of the fabric. The heading edge of the lace should be next to the raw edge of the fabric.

   b) Adjust the machine setting to a short zigzag. The zigzag should be the width of the lace heading.
   c) Zigzag the lace.
   d) Turn the lace to the right side of the fabric.
   e) Topstitch using a straight stitch.

3. Sew lace edging to the bottom of the camisole
   a) Use the same machine adjustments.
   b) Lay the right side of the lace on the right side of the fabric.

   c) The heading edge of the lace should be next to the raw edge of the fabric.

   d) Zigzag the lace and fabric together.
   e) Pull the lace down below the fabric and press.
   f) The zigzagged seam will be on the inside of the garment.
   g) Topstitch on the fabric very close to the lace using a straight stitch.

4. Press under ½" (12 mm) of fabric on each side of the center-back. Try on doll. The openings should come together at the center-back.
5. Sew hook and loop tape to the back of the camisole. (**Tips** p. 91)
6. Cut two 5" (12.5 cm) lengths of ribbon.
7. On the inside of the garment hand sew each piece of ribbon to the front of the garment where the A dots have been marked.
8. Pin the ribbon lengths to the back of the garment where the B dots have been marked. Leave about 3" (7.5 cm) of ribbon between the A and B dots to serve as shoulder straps.

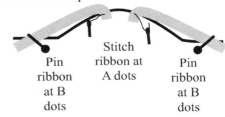

Pin ribbon at B dots   Stitch ribbon at A dots   Pin ribbon at B dots

9. Try the garment on the doll and adjust the straps.
10. Hand sew the pinned ribbon lengths to the back of the garment.
11. Sew an applique on front of camisole if desired.

Pants

1. Cut out two pants pieces from the pattern
2. Sew a lace edging on each of the two fabric pieces at A-A and at B-B. Follow the same instructions that you used for adding lace to the bottom of the camisole.

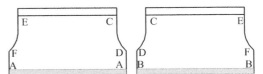

3. With right sides together, match the single notches and sew the two pieces together at C-D in the center-front of the pants.
4. Finish seam. Do not sew center-back yet.
5. Make an elastic casing at the waist at E-C-E.
    1. Finish the raw edge at the top of the pants.
    2. Press ½" (12 mm) of fabric at the top of the pants to the wrong side of the pants.
    3. Topstitch the casing ¼" to ⅜" (6 mm to 9 mm) from the folded edge.

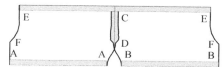

6. Insert elastic in the waist casing, pull up to 11½" (29 cm). (**Tips** p. 90)
7. With right sides together sew center-back at E-F matching the triple notches.
8. Finish seam.

9. Fold pants so that the center-front C and center-back E are touching and edges of the insides of the legs are together and ready to be sewn.
10. Sew leg seams at A-D-B.
11. Finish seam.

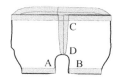

12. Turn right side out

Sandals

1. Cut out two soles and two insoles from felt.
2. Mark the line guide on the insoles.
3. Cut two 3¾" (9 cm) sandal straps from ½ to ¾" (15 to 20 mm) ribbon.
4. Line up the ribbon with the guide line. The ribbon should make a loop with the two raw edges touching. Glue a ribbon strap to each insole.
5. Glue each insole to its sole with the raw edges of the ribbons sandwiched between the insole and the sole.

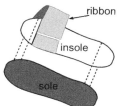

6. Use clothes pins to hold the sole in place while the glue dries.

7. Add buttons or appliques to the sandal straps if you like.

Face Page

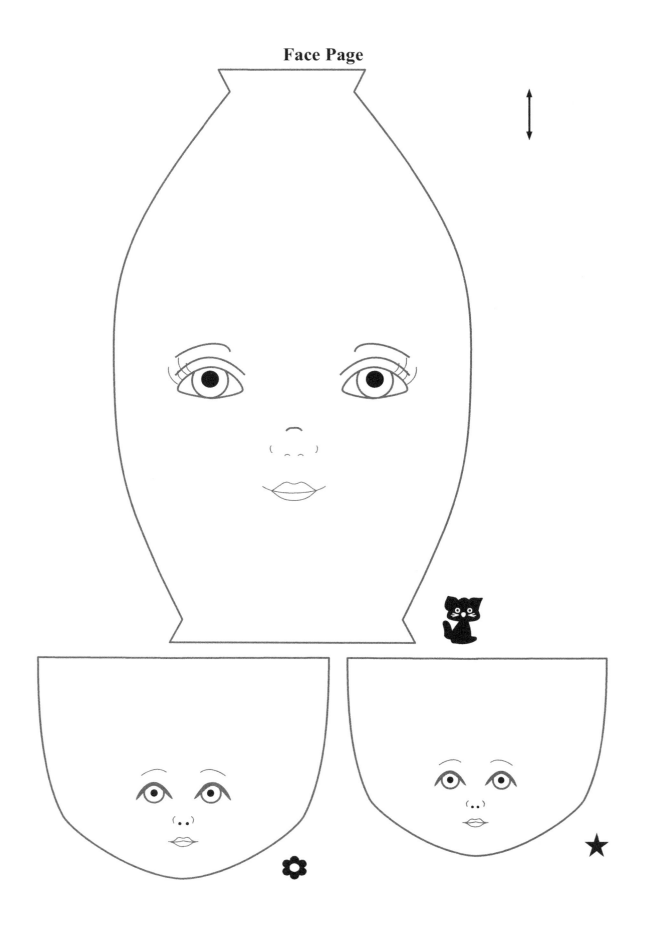

Face Page

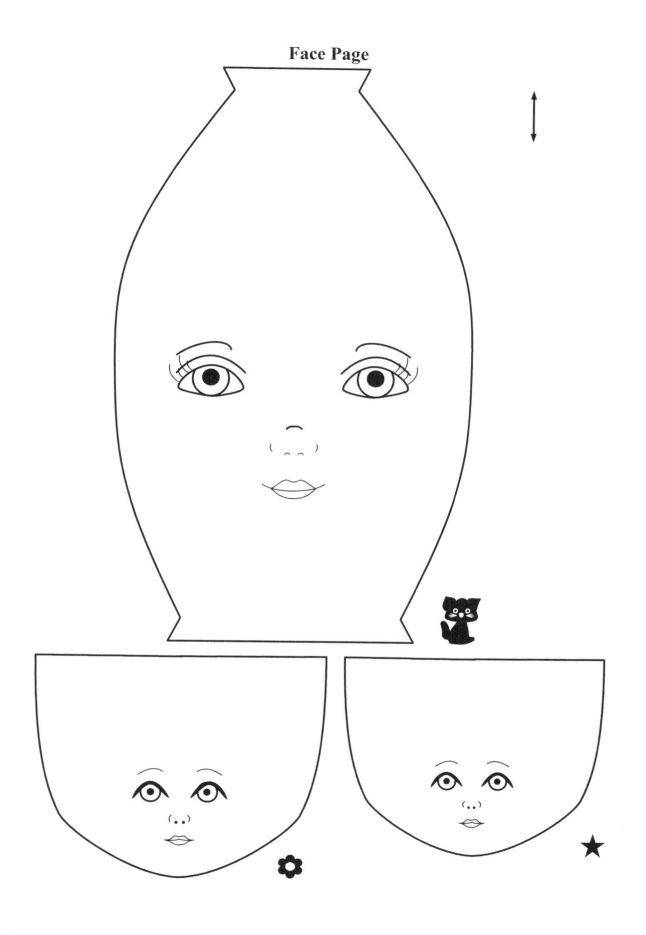

Kitty Doll

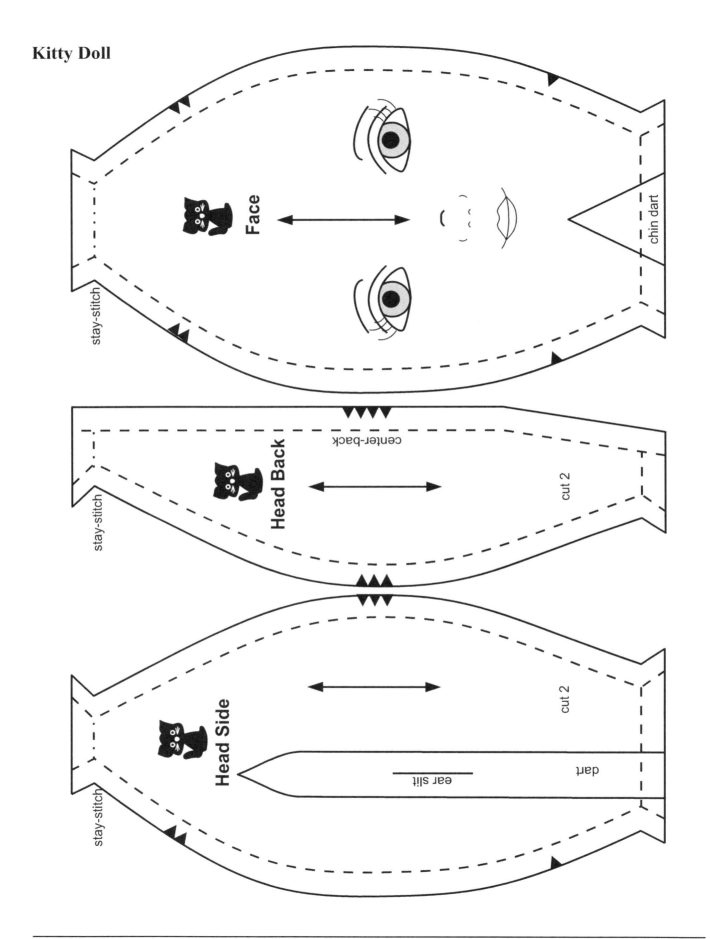

Kitty Doll

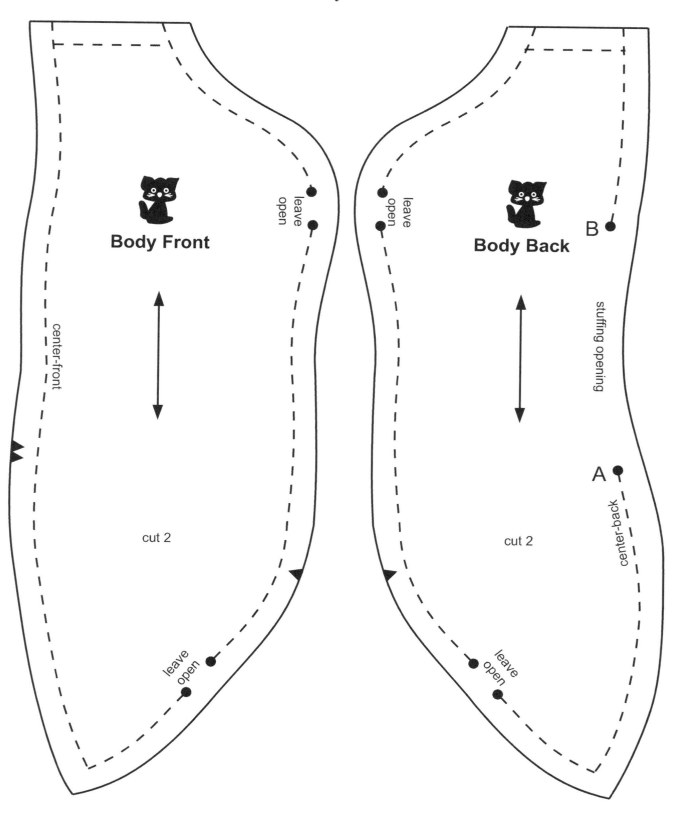

Body Front

center-front

cut 2

leave open

leave open

Body Back

stuffing opening

B

A

center-back

cut 2

leave open

leave open

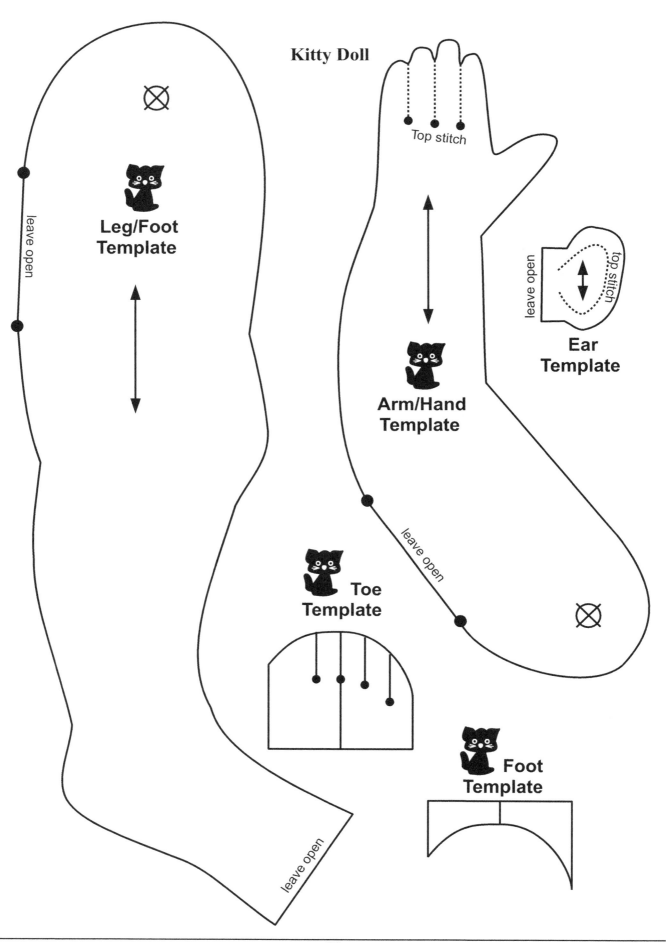

Kitty Doll

Top stitch

Leg/Foot
Template

leave open

Arm/Hand
Template

Ear
Template

leave open

top stitch

Toe
Template

leave open

Foot
Template

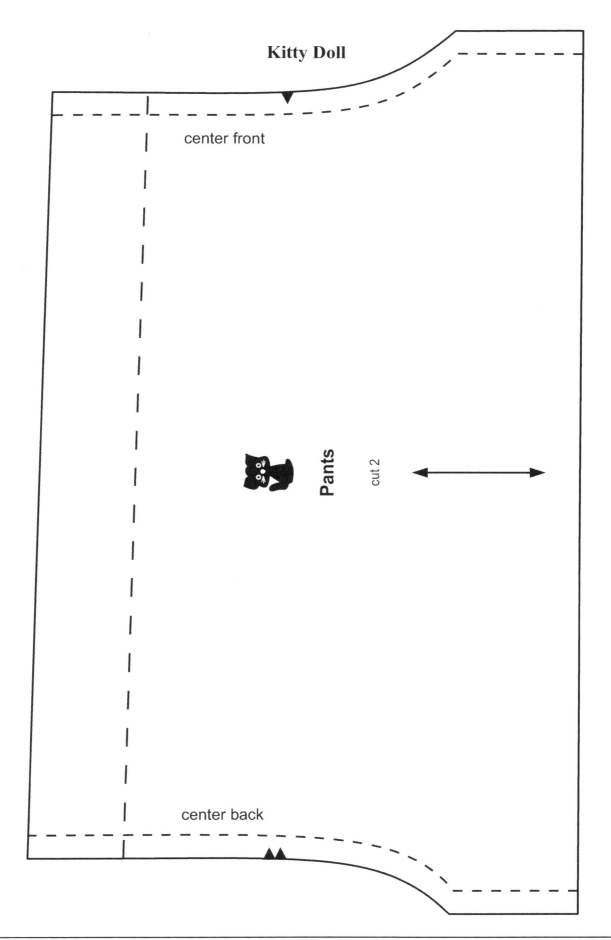

Kitty Doll

center front

Pants

cut 2

center back

Kitty Doll

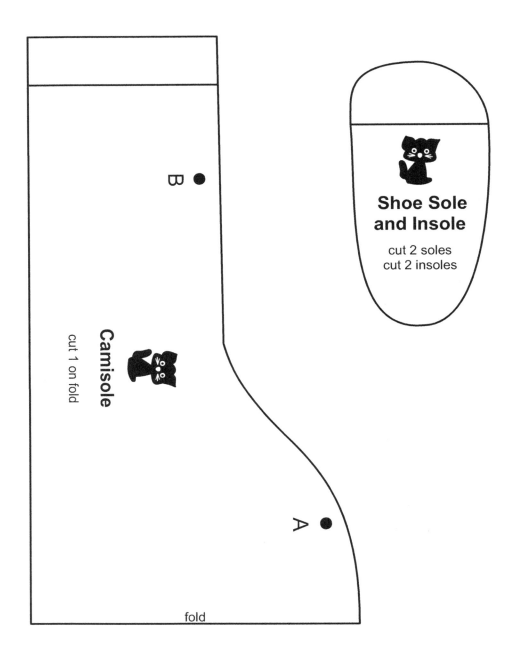

B ●

Camisole

cut 1 on fold

A ●

fold

Shoe Sole
and Insole

cut 2 soles
cut 2 insoles

Nightgown, Sleep Cap, and Six Styles of Bedroom Slippers

Equipment

- Basic sewing tools (**Tips** p. 84)

Skills

- Applying neck, sleeve, and cap bands
- Applying hook and loop tape. (**Tips** p. 91)

Sizes

This pattern fits 18" (46 cm) dolls such as: Sherralyn's Dolls Kitty, dolls from the American Girl® Collection, and the Springfield® Collection.

If you would like to make Twinkle, the mini doll Kitty is holding on the cover, the pattern is in this book's companion book, *Sewing for Mini Dolls*. Twinkle's pattern is also available at www.sherralynsdolls.com. You can find a free pattern for Kitty's stuffed cat at www.sherralynsdolls.com on Florabunda's Page.

Supplies

- ½ yd (46 cm) cotton flannel or other soft cotton fabric for nightgown
- Matching thread
- Ribbon (nightgown)
- Hook and loop tape (nightgown)
- Fleece in the color of your choice for sleep cap and bedroom slippers
- Ribbing for sleep cap band
- 1" to 1½" (2.5-3.8 cm) handmade or purchased pompom for sleep cap
- Felt in the color of your choice for slipper soles and animal ears and noses
- Air soluble pen for marking animal's facial features
- Check the chart included with the slipper instructions for eyes and nose suggestions to complete the animal slipper face

Introduction

These instructions describe the construction of a nightgown, night cap, and bedroom slippers for 18" (46 cm) dolls.

Gluing the Pattern Pieces

- Copy and cut out the two pattern pieces for the nightgown.
- Cut a rectangle for the nightgown front that measures 6¼" (16 cm) by 10" (25 cm) and a rectangle for the gown back that measures 6¾" (17 cm) by 10" (25 cm). Use grid paper if you like. Glue the gown front and back to the two rectangles. Overlap each rectangle with the pattern piece by ½" (12 mm). The length of the pattern at the center front and center back should measure 13¼" (34 cm).

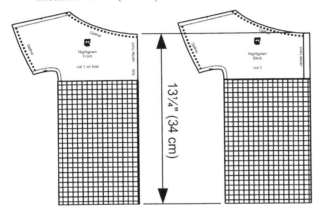

Nightgown

Cutting and Marking

- Cut one front on the fold. Cut two backs. Cut one neckband. Cut two sleeve bands.
- Mark the notches.

Sewing Shoulder/Sleeve Seams

- Match the single notches at the shoulder seam/sleeve top. Sew shoulder seams

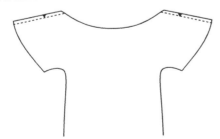

- Finish the seams.

- Open the gown out flat. Press the finished seam to the back of the garment.

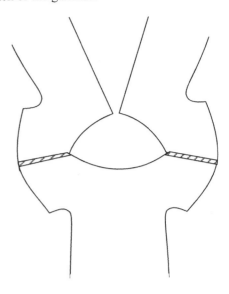

Attaching the Neckband

- Finish the raw edge on one long side of the neck band.
- With the wrong sides together, fold the neckband in half where indicated on the pattern and press.

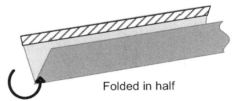

Folded in half

- Sew gathering stitches around the neck and pull up to fit the neckband.

- With right sides together, sew the unfinished edge of neckband to the gathered area of the neck.

- Slip-stitch or machine stitch the finished edge of the neckband to the neck.

Adding a Sleeve Band

- Gather the bottom of each sleeve.
- Attach the sleeve bands in the same manner that you attached the neckband.

Sides, Back, and Hem

- Fold the nightgown right sides together at the shoulder seams. Match the double notches. Sew across the bottom of each sleeve and down the garment's side. Finish the seams.

- Close the back with hook and loop tape. (**Tips** p. 91)
- Finish the raw edge of the hem.
- Press a ½ inch (12 mm) hem in the gown. Check the fit on the doll and topstitch or whip in the hem.

Sleep Cap

Cutting

- Cut one cap on the fold. Cut one cap band on the fold.

Attaching the Cap Band

- Unfold the cap band that you have just cut out.
- With the wrong sides together, fold the cap band in half lengthwise where indicated on the pattern.
- Press.
- Unfold the sleep cap.
- Place the pressed cap band on the right side of the cap bottom. Match the raw edges.
- Zigzag or serge the band to the cap.

- Pull the band down to lengthen the cap and hide the seam.

- Press lightly.

Sewing the Cap

- With right sides together, refold the cap.
- Zigzag or serge the raw edges of the cap.

Finishing the Sleep Cap

- Turn the cap right side out.
- Hand sew a pompom to the tip of the cap.

Bedroom Slippers

Cutting and Marking

- Cut two slippers from fleece.
- Cut out two soles from felt.
- Cut out four ears.
- Cut four ear inserts if needed from felt.

- Cut out two noses from felt if the animal pattern uses a felt nose.
- Mark feature placement dots with air soluble pen.

Sewing Slippers

I think that it is best to complete both slippers before adding facial features. You can more closely match the faces if you complete them at the same time.

- Stay-stitch the bottom of the slipper ¼ inch (6 mm) from the raw edge. The fabric below the stay-stitch line will be turned under and sewn to the sole.

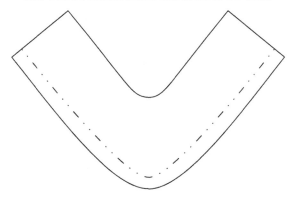

- Right sides together, bring the two short sides of the slipper together and sew.

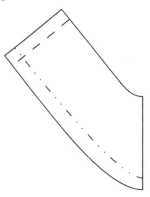

Sewing the Sole to the Vamp

In this part of the instructions the word "vamp" refers to the top part of the slipper.

- Clip the bottom of the vamp in the four places shown on the pattern. Stop each clip at the slipper's stay-stitching.

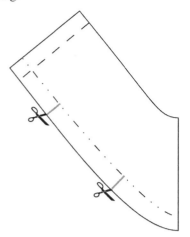

- Hand gather the toe fabric at the bottom of the vamp until it curls around the slipper's stay-stitching. The hand stitching should be very close to the cut edge.

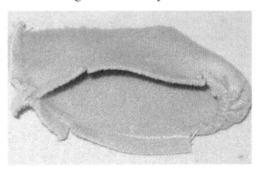

- Right sides together, match the toe of the sole to the gathered toe of the vamp. Match the single notches.
- Hand baste the gathered toe fabric to the sole.

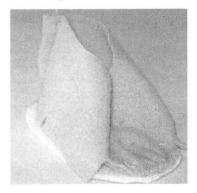

- Match the double notches on the sole to the heel seam on the vamp with a pin. Baste the sides and heel of the vamp to the sole.

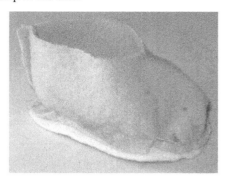

- Machine stitch the vamp to the sole on top of the stay-stitching.
- Turn right side out.

Making Facial Features

Use the chart to help with the facial features of each animal slipper, or design your own critter slipper.

Bunny	
Ears	Pleated felt, no insert
Eyes	5 mm wiggle eyes
Nose	5 mm pompom

Cat	
Ears	Glued felt, glued insert
Eyes	5 mm wiggle eyes
Nose	Glued felt
Whiskers	One strand thread
Mouth	One strand thread

Dog	
Ears	Glued felt, no insert
Eyes	7 mm wiggle eyes
Nose	Glued felt

Bear	
Ears	Glued felt, no insert
Eyes	4 mm black bead
Nose	12 mm and 5 mm pompoms

Pig	
Ears	Glued felt, no insert
Eyes	2 mm black seed bead
Nose	½" (12 mm) four hole button with black thread vertical stitching

Mouse	
Ears	Pleated felt with glued felt insert
Eyes	2 mm black bead
Nose	7 mm pompom
Whiskers	One strand thread

- Check placement dots by laying out the facial features on the slipper before gluing or sewing them down. Make adjustments where needed.
- Ears
  - Glue mouse or cat's ear inserts.

- Pleat mouse or rabbit's ears.

- Glue or sew the ears in place.

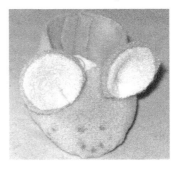

- Eyes
  - Glue eyes in place.
- Nose
  - Sew pig's button nose vertically with black thread to define nostrils.
  - Glue on pompom or felt noses.

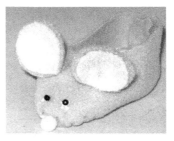

The mouse is not really sad, even though he looks like he is crying. He will look happier when the glue dries and he gets his whiskers.

- Mouth and Whiskers
  - Use large single stitches with one strand of black floss to make whiskers on the mouse and cat.

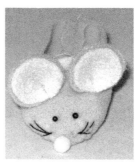

  - Use large single stitches with one strand of black floss to make the mouth on the cat slipper.

**Night gown, Sleep Cap,
and Six Pairs of Bedroom Slippers**

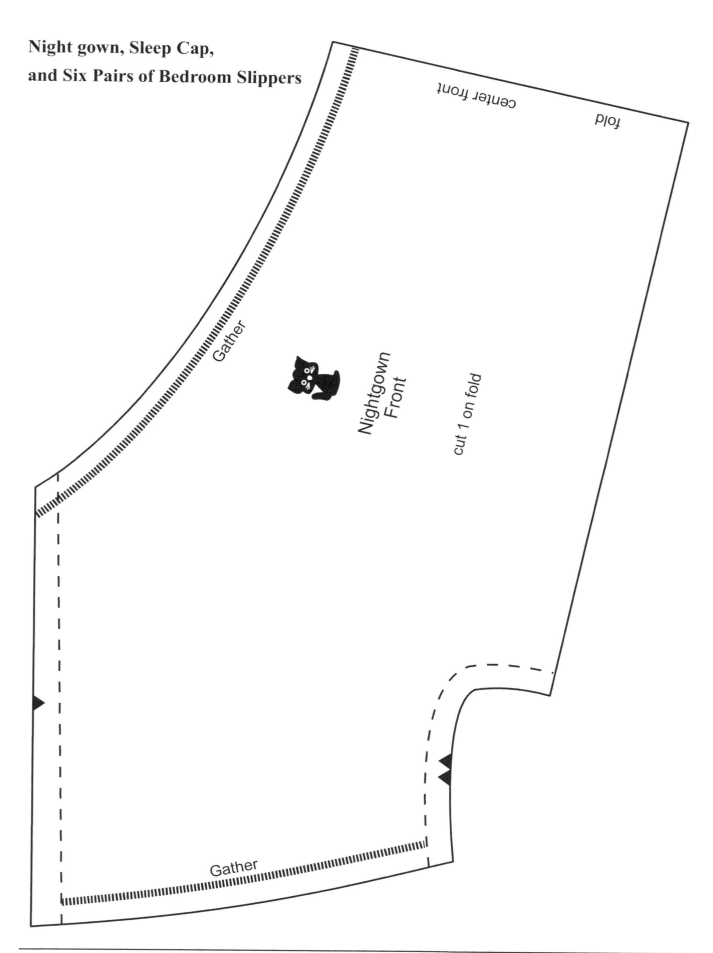

fold

center front

Nightgown
Front

cut 1 on fold

Gather

Gather

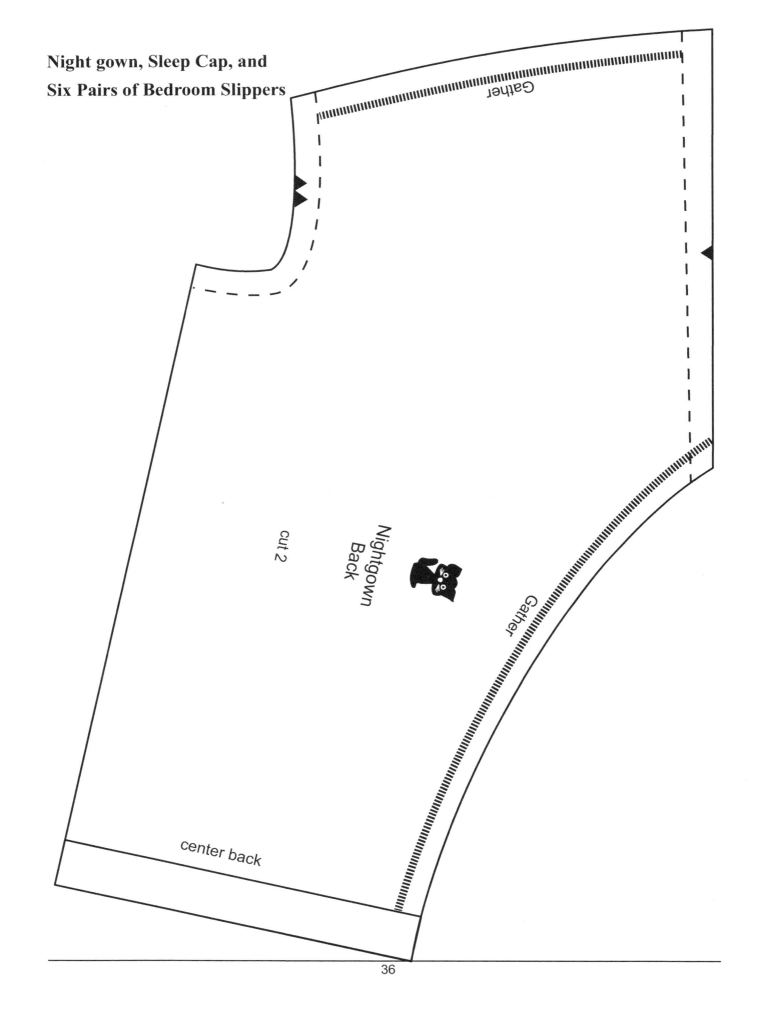

**Night gown, Sleep Cap, and
Six Pairs of Bedroom Slippers**

Gather

Gather

cut 2

Nightgown
Back

center back

36

Night gown, Sleep Cap, and Six Pairs of Bedroom Slippers

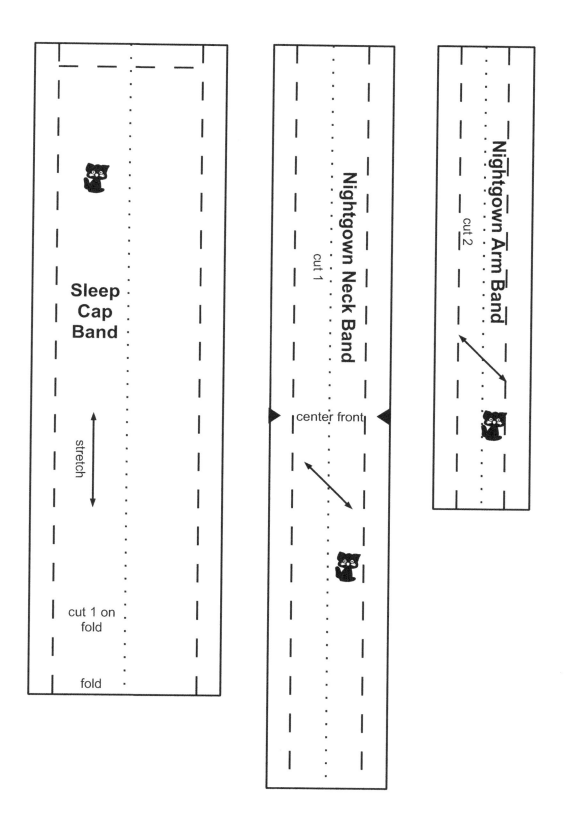

Sleep Cap Band

stretch

cut 1 on fold

fold

Nightgown Neck Band

cut 1

center front

Nightgown Arm Band

cut 2

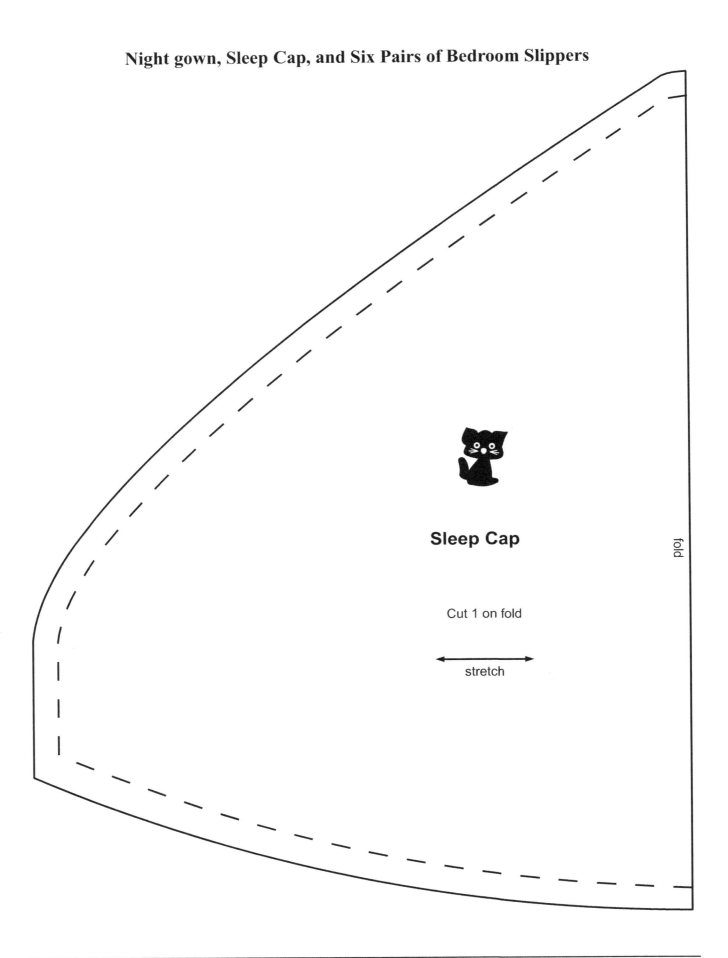

Sleep Cap

Cut 1 on fold

stretch

fold

Night gown, Sleep Cap, and Six Pairs of Bedroom Slippers

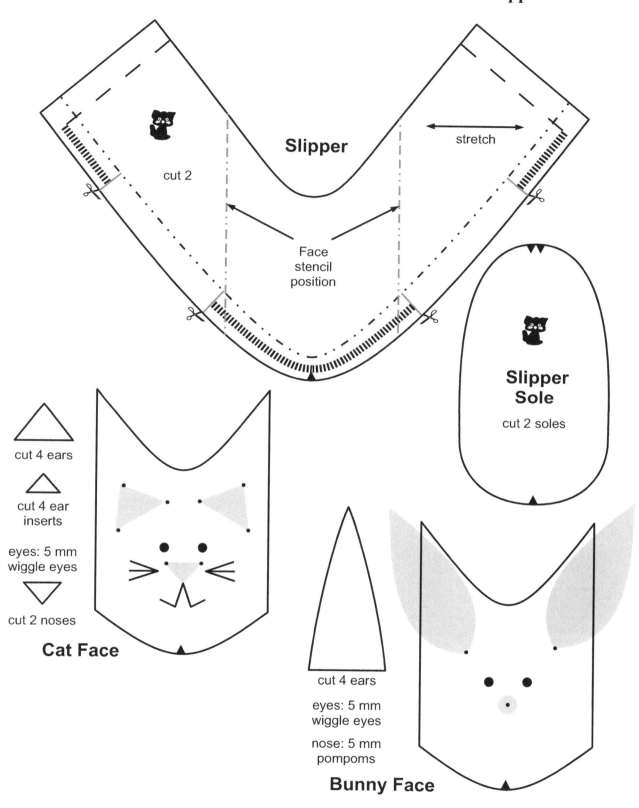

Slipper

cut 2

stretch

Face
stencil
position

**Slipper
Sole**

cut 2 soles

cut 4 ears

cut 4 ear
inserts

eyes: 5 mm
wiggle eyes

cut 2 noses

Cat Face

cut 4 ears

eyes: 5 mm
wiggle eyes

nose: 5 mm
pompoms

Bunny Face

Night gown, Sleep Cap, and Six Pairs of Bedroom Slippers

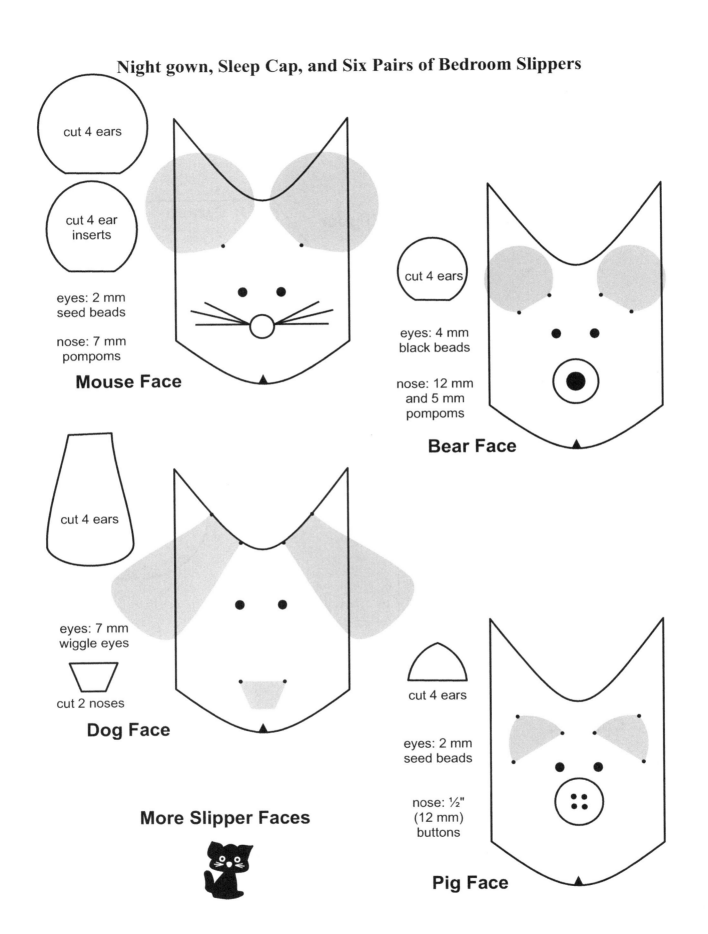

cut 4 ears

cut 4 ear inserts

eyes: 2 mm seed beads

nose: 7 mm pompoms

Mouse Face

cut 4 ears

eyes: 4 mm black beads

nose: 12 mm and 5 mm pompoms

Bear Face

cut 4 ears

eyes: 7 mm wiggle eyes

cut 2 noses

Dog Face

More Slipper Faces

cut 4 ears

eyes: 2 mm seed beads

nose: ½" (12 mm) buttons

Pig Face

A-line Dress and Short Jacket

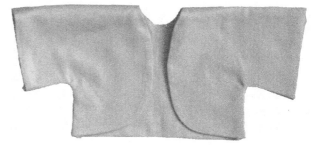

Sizes

- This pattern fits 18" (46 cm) dolls such as: Sherralyn's Dolls Kitty, dolls from the American Girl® Collection, and the Springfield® Collection.

Here is Twinkle, the mini doll Kitty is holding on the cover. The A-line dress and jacket that she is wearing, matches the A-line dress and jacket on the back cover of this book. The patterns for Twinkle and her clothing are in this book's companion book, *Sewing for Mini Dolls*. Twinkle's patterns fit American Girl® Mini dolls and are also available at www.sherralynsdolls.com.

Supplies

- ⅓ yard (30 cm) cotton fabric (dress) You can also use a fat quarter for the dress.
- Cotton fabric to match or complement A-line dress (jacket)
- Matching thread
- Hook and loop tape for closing back

Equipment

- Basic sewing tools (**Tips** p. 84)

Skills

- Dress
  - Applying a facing to both neck opening and armholes (explained in the instructions)
- Jacket
  - Lining a jacket

Introduction

These instructions describe the construction of an A-line dress and jacket for 18" (46 cm) dolls.

A-line Dress

Cutting and Marking

- Cut one front and one front facing on fold. Cut two backs and two back facings.
- Mark the notches.

Applying Facing

- Right sides together, match the single notches and sew the dress front to the dress backs at the shoulders.
- Press the seams open.
- Right sides together, match the single notches and sew the facing front to the facing backs at the shoulders.
- Press the seams open.
- Finish the bottom of front and back facings.
- Right sides together, lay the facing on the dress matching neck, armholes, and back openings.
- Sew all the way around the neck and then around each armhole.

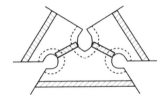

- Trim the seam to ⅛".
- Turn the dress right side out by pulling the facing through the space at each shoulder between the neck and armhole of the dress and facing, as shown in the following pictures:
- Prepare to turn the dress right side out.

- Pull one back panel through its shoulder space.

- Continue pulling until the first back panel and facing are pulled through.

- Then pull second back panel and facing through the second opening.
- The photo below shows the wrong side of the dress when both backs and facings have been pulled through the correct shoulder opening.

- Press.
- Top stitch around neck and armholes (optional).

Sewing Side Seams

- Fold the dress at the shoulders right sides together. Match the double notches at the side seams.
- Sew side seams.
- Finish side seams.

- Turn right side out.
- Press.

Back Openings

- I like to close this dress with a flat back seam the way the back opening would close with a zipper. I always leave a ½" (12 mm) seam allowance for the back opening of my doll dress patterns instead of the ¼" (6 mm) seam allowance used for the other seams in the pattern. This extra width should make attaching hook and loop tape easier and is available to help adjust the fit of the dress.
- If you prefer, you can apply hook and loop tape all the way down the dress back instead of sewing the lower center back closed.
- Finish each of the raw edges of the back opening. Finish the raw edges at the very end of the seam allowance, so that the total seam allowance will be available.
- Pin the back closed.
- Measure 7½" (19 cm) down from the top of the back opening and mark.
- Start at the top of the opening. Sew a ½" (12 mm) seam with a machine basting stitch. At the 7½" (19 cm) mark shorten the machine stitch length and continue sewing to the bottom of the dress.

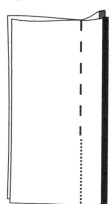

- Press the seam open and remove the basting stitches from the top 7½" (19 cm) of the seam.

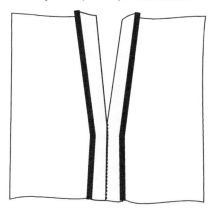

- Try the garment on the doll and make any adjustments needed.
- Apply hook and loop tape. (**Tips** p. 91) Start with the third bullet point under *Closing the Back with Hook and Loop Tape*, if you have sewn the lower back closed.

Hem

- Finish the bottom edge of the dress.
- Run a gathering stitch around the finished bottom edge of the dress.
- Press a ½" (12 mm) hem in the dress. Try on the dress and check the hem on the doll.
- Pull the gathering stitch so that the hem lies flat inside the dress.
- Slip-stitch the hem.

Decorations

- If you like, add buttons or small appliques at the center front.

Short Jacket

Cutting and Marking

- Cut two fronts and two front linings.
- Cut one back and one back lining on fold.
- Mark the notches.

Lining the Jacket

- Match single notches at shoulder/sleeve top of jacket.
- Sew jacket together at shoulder/sleeve top.

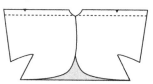

- Press seams open.
- Sew the same seams on lining.
- Press seams open.

- Right sides together, pin or baste jacket to the lining.
- Sew jacket front, the bottom of jacket back, and the edges of the sleeves to the lining.

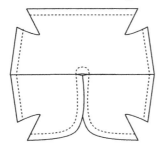

- Clip corners and curves.

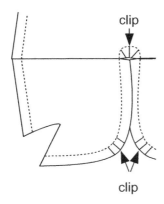

- Turn jacket right side out through one unsewn side. The following picture shows the unturned jacket:

○ Begin pulling one side through a side opening.

○ Continue pulling the jacket through the opening.

○ Finish turning jacket.

- Press.

- Fold jacket right sides together at shoulder/sleeve seam.

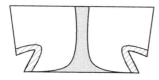

- Match double notches.
- Sew around sleeve bottoms and jacket sides.
- Finish seams.
- Turn right side out.
- Press.
- Topstitch around the outside of the jacket (optional).

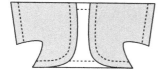

A-line Dress and Short Jacket

center front

A-Line Dress Front

cut 1 on fold

fold

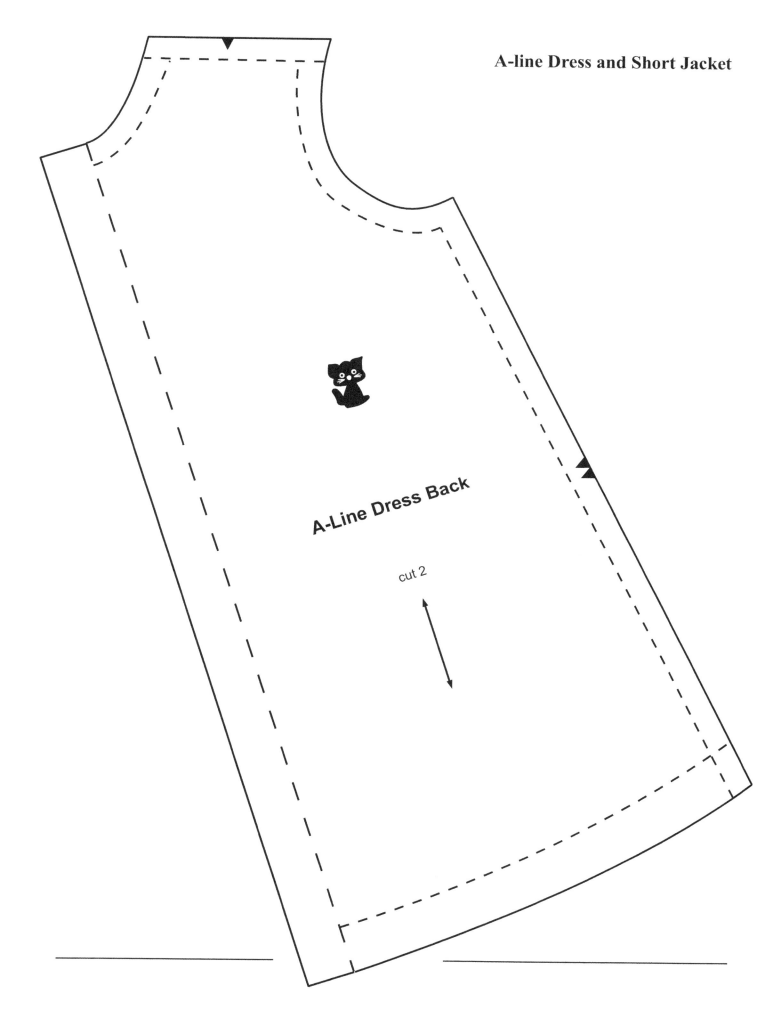

A-line Dress and Short Jacket

A-Line Dress Back

cut 2

A-line Dress and Short Jacket

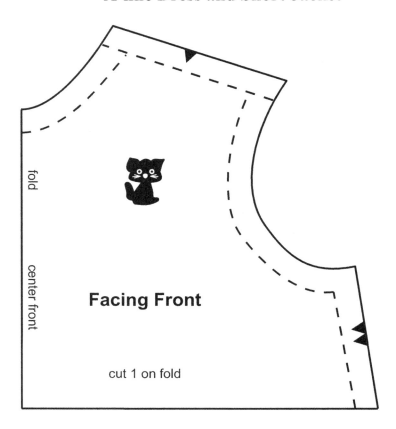

fold

center front

Facing Front

cut 1 on fold

Facing Back

cut 2

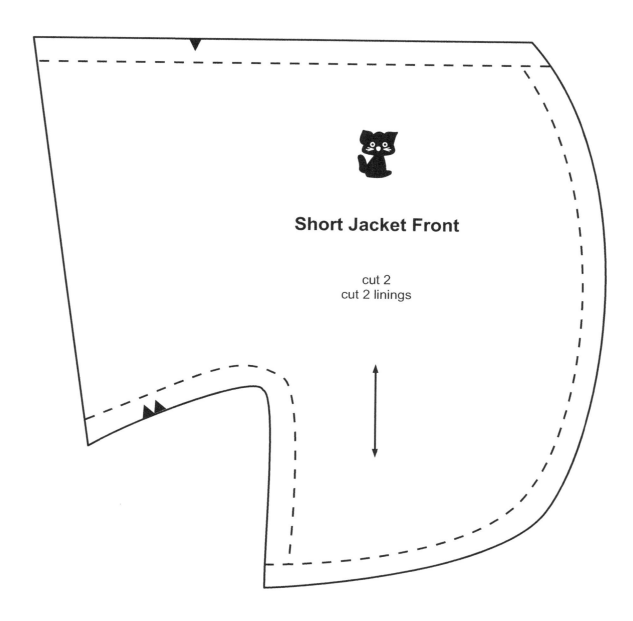

Short Jacket Front

cut 2
cut 2 linings

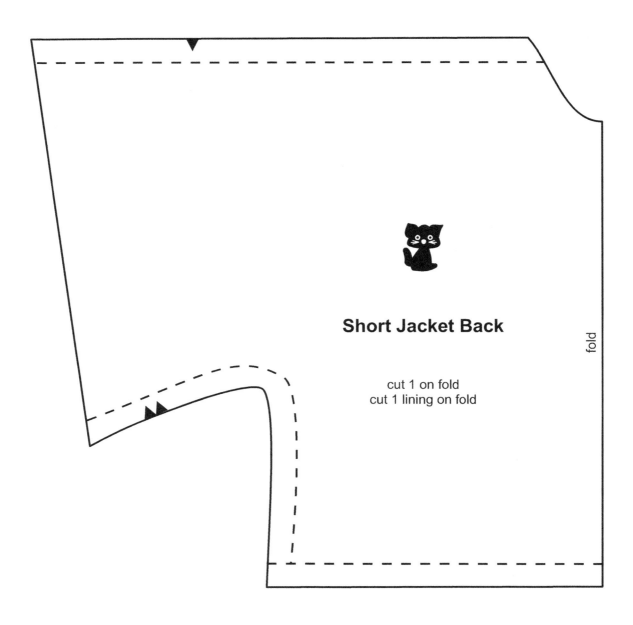

Short Jacket Back

cut 1 on fold
cut 1 lining on fold

fold

Pants, T-Shirt, Skirt, and Sneakers

Supplies

- Pants, shorts, and skirt
  - Chambray, light denim, or cotton broadcloth in color of your choice for pants, shorts, and skirt
  - Matching thread and optional orange thread for jeans topstitching
  - Sewing glue stick for pockets (optional)
- ⅛" (3 mm) elastic for waist casing
- T-shirt
  - Knit fabric in color of your choice
  - Matching or contrasting ribbing
  - Matching thread
  - Hook and loop tape
- Sneakers
  - Light weight denim or cotton broadcloth in the color of your choice for sneakers and a scrap of white or contrasting fabric for the optional toe overlay
  - ¼" (6 mm) elastic for band above sneaker sole
  - Seam sealant
  - Stiff felt for insole
  - White craft foam sheet for sole
  - Tacky Glue®
  - Midi braid for laces
- Socks
  - A thin sock or ribbing knit fabric

Equipment

- Basic sewing tools (**Tips** p. 84)
- Cotton swabs to hold shoe eyelets open
- Spring clothes pins for holding soles to shoes
- Pennies or other weights

Skills

- Pants and skirt
  - Applying a patch pocket to pants and skirt to make jeans and khakis
- T-shirt
  - Attaching a neck band (explained in the instructions)
  - Sewing knit with a zigzag stitch (explained in the instructions)
  - Setting-in a sleeve (explained in the instructions)
  - Applying hook and loop tape (**Tips** p. 91)

Sizes

This pattern fits 18" (46 cm) dolls such as: Sherralyn's Dolls Kitty, dolls from the American Girl® Collection, and the Springfield® Collection

Here is Twinkle, the mini doll Kitty is holding on the cover. She is wearing a T-shirt, jeans and sneakers. The patterns for Twinkle and her clothing are in this book's companion book, *Sewing for Mini Dolls*. Twinkle's patterns fit American Girl® Mini dolls and are also available at www.sherralynsdolls.com.

Introduction

These instructions describe the construction of long pants, shorts, A-line skirt, optional pockets, a T-shirt, and sneakers with socks for 18" (46 cm) dolls.

Applying Patch Pockets for Pants or Skirt

If you are planning to make pants or a skirt with pockets, start here. If you are making your project without pockets, start at the **Pants and Shorts** section or the **Skirt** section. This method of applying pockets makes it easier to produce pockets of a consistent size and shape.

Cutting and Marking

- Cut two of the jeans or shorts fronts and two of the jeans or shorts backs; or cut one front and one back skirt from the skirt pattern.
- Mark the notches.

Sewing the Pockets

- Fold a scrap of fabric in half right, sides together.
- Draw two pockets on the folded fabric by tracing around the pants or skirt pocket template. If you have freezer paper, you can trace your template onto a piece of freezer paper. Cut out the tracing and iron the waxy side of the tracing onto your fabric instead of drawing the pocket on the fabric. The freezer paper method saves time. I have been able to reuse my freezer paper tracing at least three times.
- Sew on the traced lines or the outside edge of the freezer paper, but leave the top and side of each pocket open.
- Cut out pockets using a ⅛" (3 mm) seam allowance.

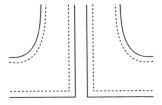

- Turn pockets right side out and press.
- Topstitch the curved area that will be left open when the pocket is sewn to the pants or skirt. Use gold or orange thread for jeans if you like.

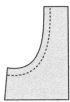

Attaching the Pockets

- Use air soluble pen to mark the pocket placement on the right side of both pants front pieces or mark two pockets on the skirt front. If you are making a skirt,

mark the pockets on only one cut skirt piece. The pockets will define the skirt front.
- Place pockets over placement markings.
- Pin in place or use sewing glue stick.
- Topstitch around the two straight areas that will not be caught in the seam. Use orange or gold thread for jeans if you like.

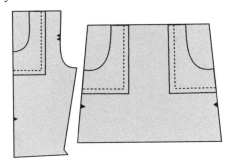

Go to the section titled: Sewing the Side Seams if you are sewing pants. Go to the section titled: Making the Casing and Inserting Elastic if you are making a skirt.

Pants and Shorts

Cutting and Marking

- Cut two of the jeans or shorts fronts and two of the jeans or shorts backs.
- Mark the notches.

Sewing the Side Seams

- Match the side of each pants front to the side of a pants back. Match the single notches.
- Sew the side seams. The raw edges of the pockets should be caught in the seams.
- Finish the side seams. Finish the two raw edges together by zigzagging or serging, so that they can be pressed in one direction. If the seam is pressed open, it will be difficult to insert the elastic once the casing is constructed.

Sewing the Center Front Seam

- Match the double notches and sew the center fronts together.
- Finish the seam with the two raw edges together as you did with the side seams.

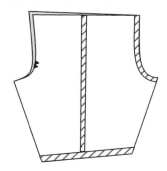

- Press the center front seam and the side seams in the same direction. You can also glue the three seams to the pants fabric at the casing area, if you have a fabric glue stick. You might find it easier to insert elastic into the finished casing if the seams are glued down.

Finishing the Pants Leg Bottoms

- Finish the raw edges at the bottom of each leg.
- Turn ¼" (6 mm) to the inside at each leg bottom and press.
- Topstitch.

Making the Casing and Inserting Elastic

- Finish the raw edge at the top of the waist. Press the fabric ½" (12mm) to the inside.
- Topstitch ¼" to ⅜" (6 to 9 mm) from the folded edge at the top of the pants to make the casing.
- Insert the elastic into the casing. Sew one end of the elastic along the raw edge of the casing.

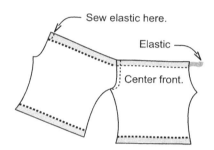

Sew elastic here.

Elastic

Center front.

- Gather the casing fabric to about 10" (25 cm) over the elastic without stretching the elastic.
- Try the pants around the doll's waist and adjust if necessary. Secure the second side of the elastic and cut off the excess.

Finishing the Pants

- Match the triple notches and sew center backs together.

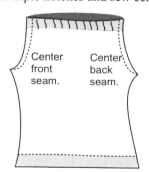

Center front seam.

Center back seam.

- Bring the center fronts and center backs together and sew the inside leg seams.

- Turn right side out.

Skirt

Cutting and Marking

- Cut one front and one back skirt from the skirt pattern.
- Mark the notches.

Making the Casing and Inserting Elastic

- Sew one side of the skirt front to the skirt back matching the single notches.
- Finish the seam. Finish the two raw edges together, so that they can be pressed in one direction. If the seam is pressed open, it will be difficult to insert the elastic once the casing is constructed.
- To make the casing, open the skirt out and finish the raw edge at the top of the waist.
- Press the fabric ½" (12 mm) to the inside.
- Top stitch ¼" to ⅜" (6 to 9 mm) from the folded edge at the top of the skirt.
- Insert the elastic into the casing. Sew one end of the elastic along a raw edge of the casing opening.

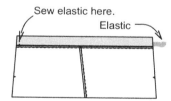

Sew elastic here.

Elastic

- Gather the casing fabric to about 10" (25 cm) over the elastic without stretching the elastic.
- Try the skirt around the doll's waist and adjust if necessary. Secure the second side of the elastic and cut off the excess.

Finishing the Skirt

- Finish the raw edge at the bottom of the skirt.
- If you would like to topstitch the hem, press the hem ½" (12 mm) to the inside and topstitch before sewing the second side seam.
- Sew the second side of skirt front to skirt back, matching single notches.
- Finish the side seam.
- If you plan to slip-stitch the hem, press the hem ½" (12 mm) to the inside and slip-stitch.

- Turn right side out.

T-shirt

Cutting and Marking

- Cut one front on fold, two backs, two sleeves, and one neck ribbing.
- Check arrows before cutting to make certain the patterns are aligned correctly with the fabric's stretch.
- Mark the dot on the sleeves.

Sewing Knit with Zigzag Seams

- If you use your machine for the T-shirt, use a zigzag stitch. If you have a serger, you can use it on this size T-shirt.
- Use a fairly wide zigzag stitch to join knits. Set the zigzags to be fairly close together.
- Note that the seam allowance is only ⅛" (3 mm).

Sewing the Shoulder Seams

- Right sides together, match the front and back single notches at shoulder seams.
- Sew the shoulder seams.

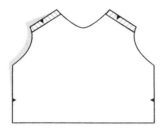

Attaching the Neckband

- Fold the ribbing in half with wrong sides together.
- Press.
- Place the folded ribbing on the right side of the shirt with the raw edges next to the neck raw edge.
- Do not fold the back closing to the inside until the ribbing has been sown to the neck. Start applying the ribbing at the raw edge of the shirt back.
- Stretch the ribbing with gentle, consistent pressure while zigzagging it to the neck. The ribbing must be stretched to fit the neck. Be careful not to stretch the fabric at the neck opening.

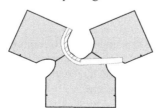

If you are using a serger, you can use it to finish the raw edge of the sleeve hem, bottom hem, and the raw edges of the back openings. Then zigzag the hem with your sewing machine. You can use your serger to sew the side seams, but use your regular machine to sew hems and hook and loop tape.

Setting in Sleeves

- Press the sleeve hem ¼" (6mm) to the inside of the fabric and zigzag.
- Match the dot at the top of the sleeve to the shoulder seam and pin the sleeve to the shoulder seam at the dot.
- Start at one side and stretch and sew the sleeve until you reach the pin at the shoulder seam/sleeve dot. Do not stretch the arm opening. Remove the pin and continue stretching the sleeve to fit the opening until you have finished sewing the sleeve.

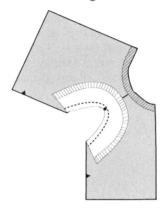

- Sew in the second sleeve.

Finishing the T-shirt

- Match the single notches on the shirt sides and zigzag across the sleeves and down the sides.
- Press the T-shirt hem and zigzag.

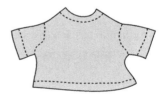

- Press both back openings ½" (12 mm) under.
- Apply hook and loop tape to back openings. (**Tips** p. 91)
- Press the hem at the bottom of the T-shirt ½" (12 mm) to the inside and zigzag the hem.

Sneakers

Marking, Sewing, and Cutting out Templates

- For a pair of sneakers, draw two sneaker sides and two sneaker tongue/toes on folded fabric by tracing around the sneaker parts templates. If you prefer, you can use the freezer paper method discussed in the pocket instructions.

- Sew around the templates. Notice the "leave open" areas marked on the templates. Do not sew between these dots.
- Cut out the sewn shoe pieces. Leave an ⅛" (3 mm) seam allowance around the stitching. If you are using freezer paper, do not remove the paper until you have cut out the pieces, so that you have a guide for cutting the "leave open" areas.
- Clip the shoe pieces where indicated in the illustrations.

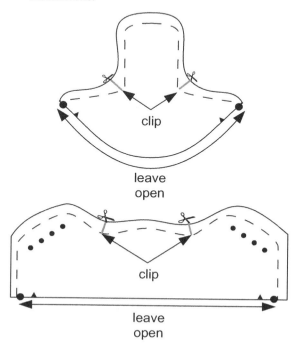

- Turn the shoe pieces right side out.
- Press.

Adding Optional Overlay

- Cut two overlays on the fold from white or contrasting fabric, if you like.
- Lay the overlay on top of the tongue/toe piece, matching the curve and single notch.
- Sew the overlay ⅛" (3 mm) from the folded edge.

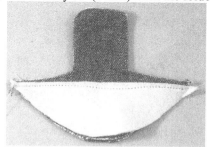

Stay-stitching the Raw Edges

- Stay stitch ¼" (6 mm) from the raw edges of the shoe sides and the tongue/toe.

Making Eyelets for the Shoe Laces

- Mark eyelet placement on the sneaker sides.
- Carefully punch out eyelet holes using an awl, ice pick, or large needle. (This step is for adults only—watch your fingers.)
- Cut four cotton swabs in half and insert one piece into each eyelet hole.
- Use seam sealant around each hole and allow it to dry.

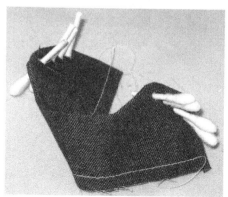

Adding Optional Topstitching

- Add optional topstitching if desired. Sew ⅛" (3 mm) around the finished edge of the shoe side. Sew a straight seam to the left or right of the eyelets.

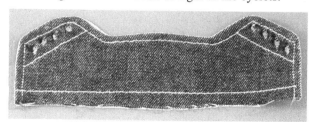

Sewing Shoe Sides to Tongue/Toe

- Mark sneaker side placement on tongue/toe piece. The placement marks are indicated by . . _ _ _ Match the single notches of one shoe side to the tongue/toe.
- Sew one shoe side to the tongue/toe. Sew the side to the tongue/toe on the line indicated on the shoe side template. If you have added topstitching to the sides, this seam will be on top of a short section of the topstitching.

- Sew the second shoe side to the tongue/toe.

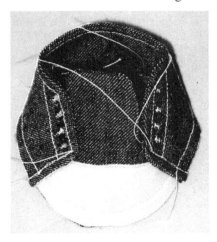

Gluing the Sole and Insole

In this part of the instructions the word "vamp" refers to the assembled sneaker side and tongue/toe.

- Cut two insoles from stiff felt. Cut two soles from a craft foam sheet. The sole is not symetric. Be sure to flip one of the soles so that you will have a left and right shoe.
- Clip the bottom of the vamp in the four places shown on the figure. Stop each clip at the vamp's stay stitching.

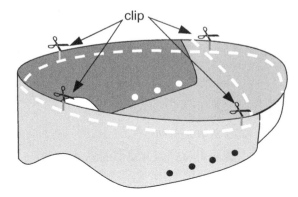

- Hand stitch toe fabric at the bottom of the vamp very close to the raw edge. Gather the stitches until the bottom of the toe fabric curls around the vamp's stay stitching.
- Insert insole into the vamp.

- Glue the gathered toe fabric to the insole.

- Hold the ungathered sides of the vamp to the insole with spring clothes pins while you work on the heel.

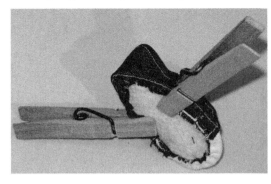

- Hand stitch heel fabric at the bottom of the vamp very close to the cut edge. Gather the stitches until the bottom of the heel fabric curls around the vamp's stay stitching.
- Glue the gathered heel fabric to the insole.
- Remove the clothes pins and glue the vamp's sides to the insole from the stay-stitching to the raw edge.

- Glue the sole to the outside of the vamp against the insole, hiding the insole and the vamp's raw edges.

- Put weights (I used pennies) inside the shoe and allow the glue to dry.

Adding a Band above the Shoe Sole

- Cut two strips of ¼" (6 mm) elastic using the sneaker strip guide.
- Start at the shoe's heel. Glue the elastic around the bottom of the sneaker.
- Stretch the elastic gently at the toe for a good fit.
- Overlap the elastic slightly at the heel and cut off any extra elastic.
- A large rubber band will hold the elastic in place while the glue dries, if you need it.

Making Shoe Laces

- Cut two 17" (42 cm) lengths of midi braid.
- Dip each braid end in glue.
- While the glue is still wet, twist each end of the braid tightly until it resembles the tip of a shoe lace.

- When the glue has dried, insert the lace into the sneakers.

Sock

Cutting and Marking

- Cut socks on the fold.
- If you are using a sock for your source of knit fabric, you can place the top of the sock pattern at the finished top of your sock. Then you can skip the *Finishing the Top* section of the instructions and go straight to *Sewing the Sock*.

Finishing the Top

- To finish the top, open the folded fabric and turn ⅛" (3 cm) of fabric to the wrong side of the sock and zigzag.

- You may zigzag narrow lace to the sock instead of hemming if you like. For a lettuce edge stretch the knit fabric as you attach the lace.

Sewing the Sock

- Refold each sock so that the right sides are together.

- Use a narrow zigzag stitch to sew from the top of the sock down the side and around the foot to the toe.

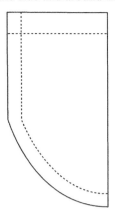

- Turn the sock right side out.

Pants, T-Shirt, and Skirt

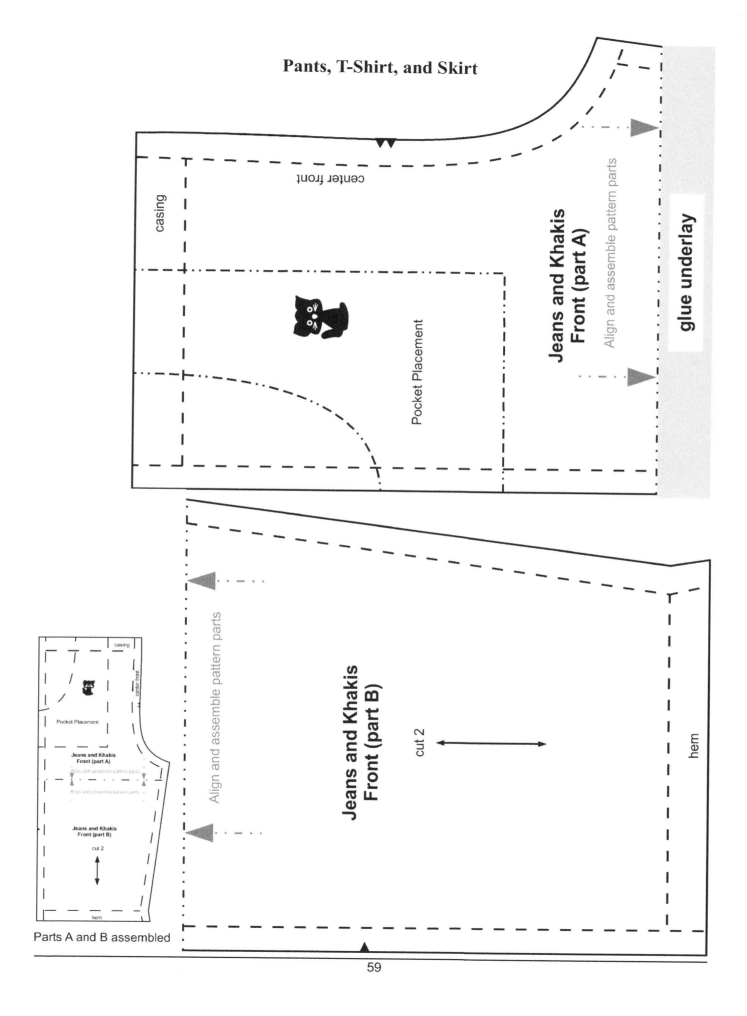

casing

center front

Jeans and Khakis
Front (part A)

Align and assemble pattern parts

Pocket Placement

glue underlay

Jeans and Khakis
Front (part B)

Align and assemble pattern parts

cut 2

hem

Parts A and B assembled

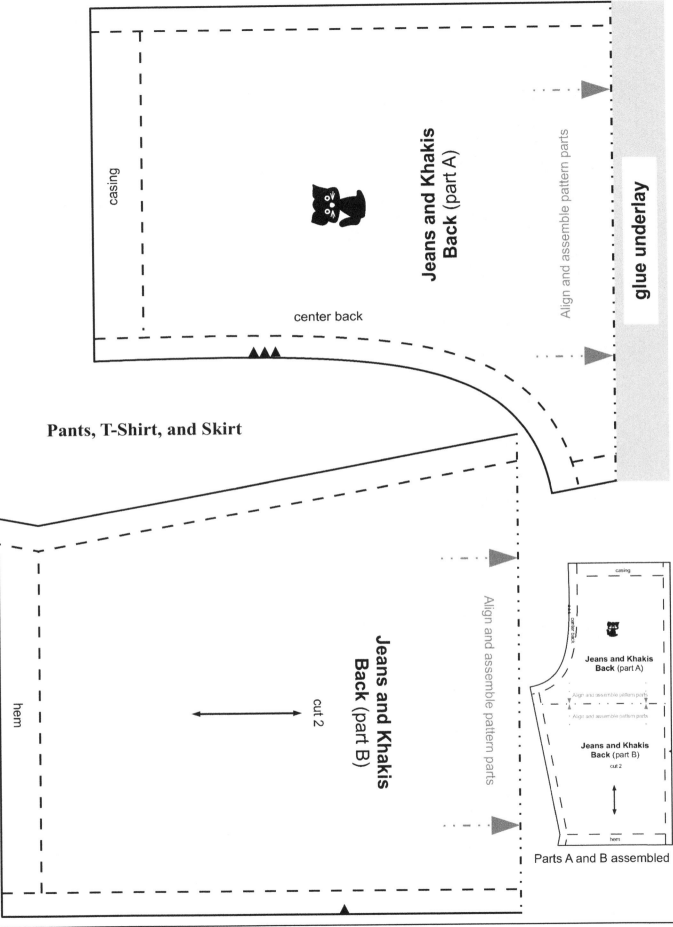

casing

Jeans and Khakis Back (part A)

Align and assemble pattern parts

glue underlay

center back

Pants, T-Shirt, and Skirt

hem

Jeans and Khakis Back (part B)

cut 2

Align and assemble pattern parts

casing

center back

Jeans and Khakis Back (part A)

Align and assemble pattern parts

Align and assemble pattern parts

Jeans and Khakis Back (part B)

cut 2

hem

Parts A and B assembled

Pants, T-Shirt, and Skirt

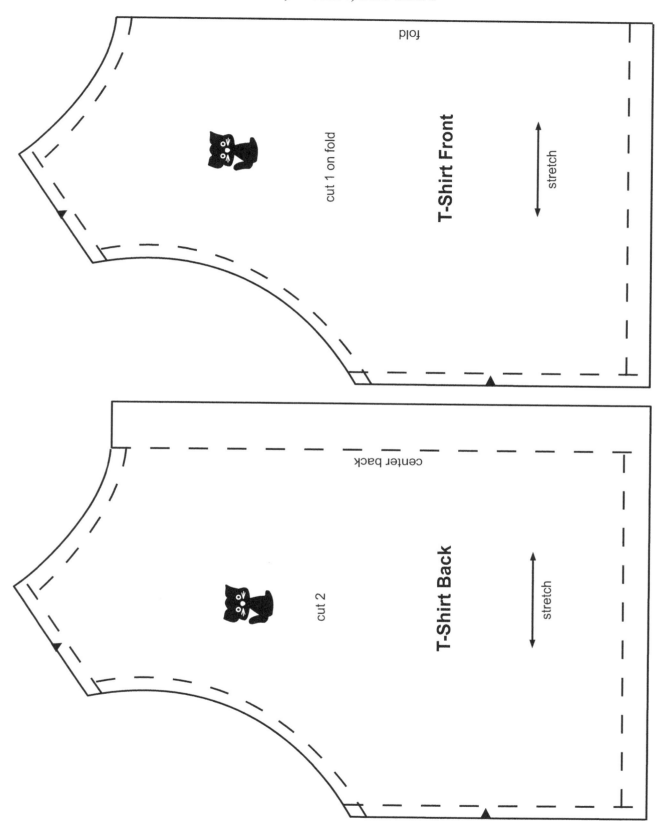

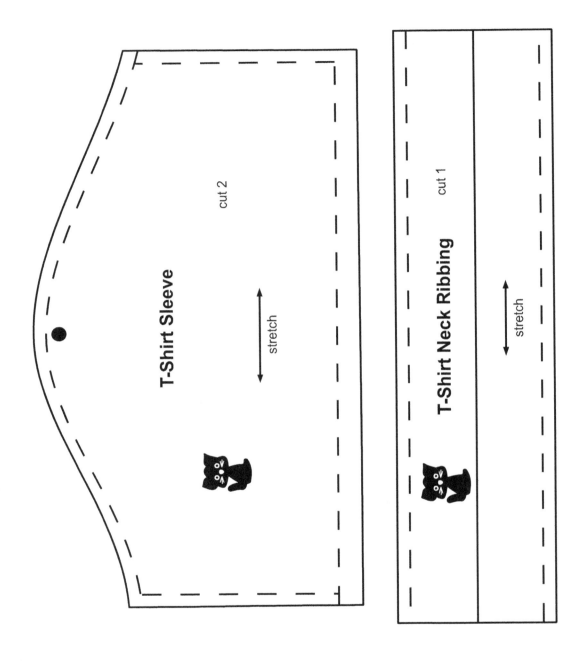

T-Shirt Sleeve

cut 2

stretch

T-Shirt Neck Ribbing

cut 1

stretch

Pants, T-Shirt, and Skirt

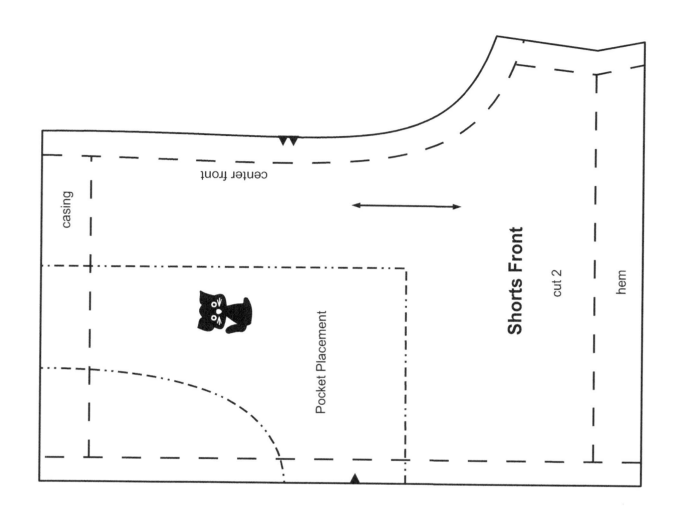

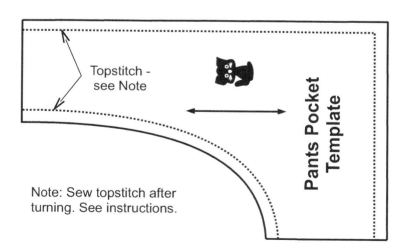

Note: Sew topstitch after turning. See instructions.

Pants, T-Shirt, and Skirt

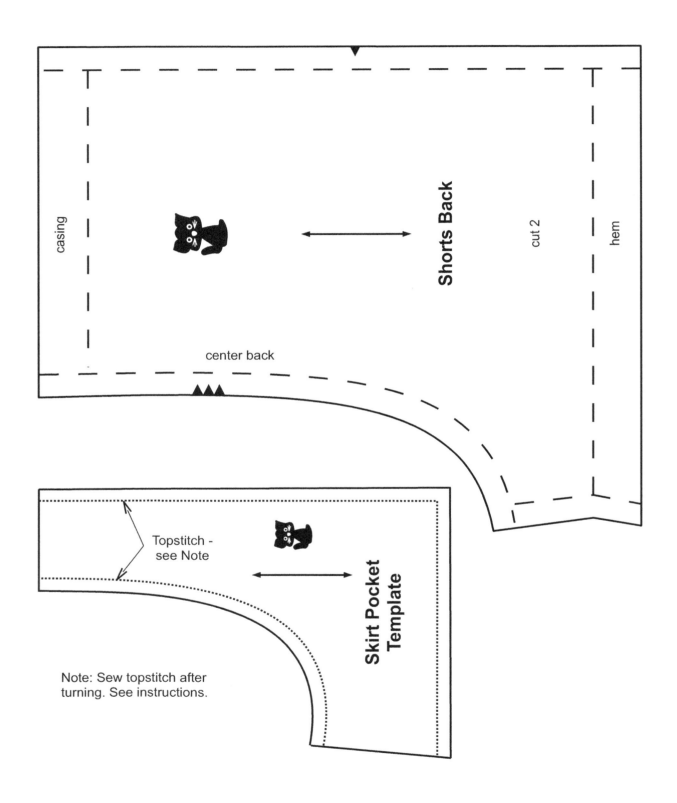

casing

Shorts Back

cut 2

hem

center back

Topstitch - see Note

Skirt Pocket Template

Note: Sew topstitch after turning. See instructions.

Pants, T-Shirt, and Skirt

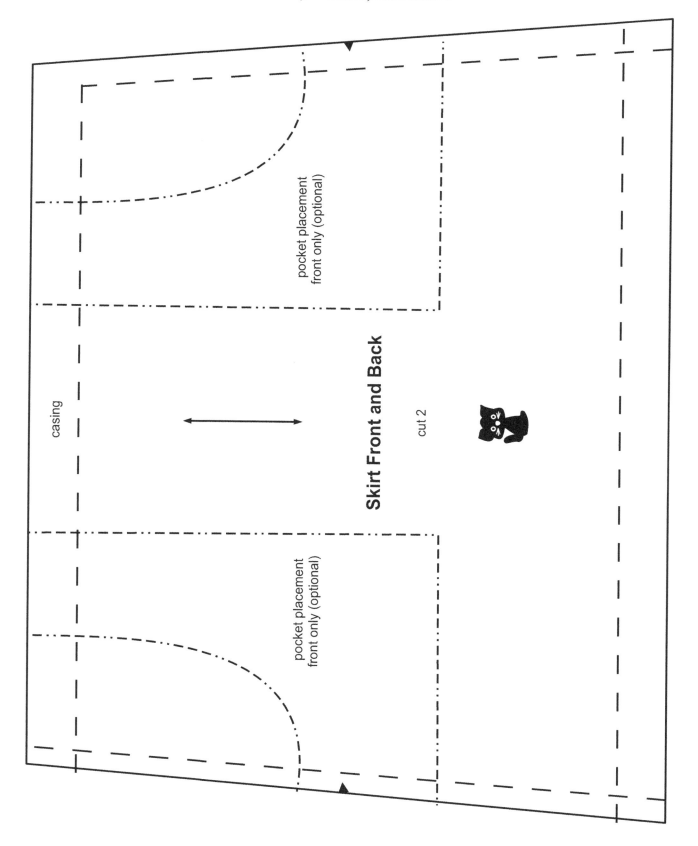

pocket placement
front only (optional)

pocket placement
front only (optional)

casing

Skirt Front and Back

cut 2

Pants, T-Shirt, and Skirt

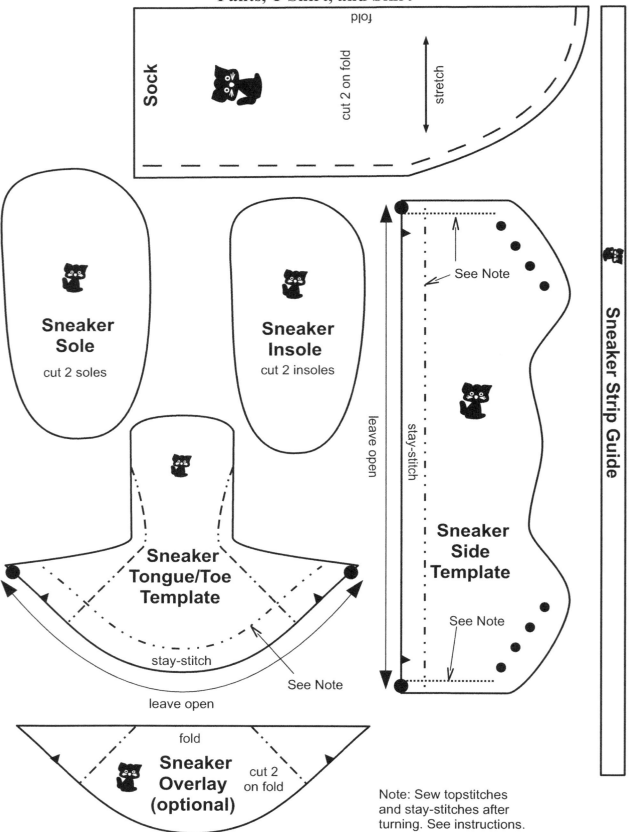

Sock

fold

cut 2 on fold

stretch

Sneaker Sole

cut 2 soles

Sneaker Insole

cut 2 insoles

Sneaker Strip Guide

See Note

stay-stitch

Sneaker Side Template

See Note

leave open

Sneaker Tongue/Toe Template

stay-stitch

See Note

leave open

fold

Sneaker Overlay (optional)

cut 2 on fold

Note: Sew topstitches and stay-stitches after turning. See instructions.

Ballgown and Classic Dress with Accessories

Supplies

- Dresses
  - ¼ yd (23 cm) cotton fabric for bodice and skirt of classic dress
  - A large scrap of cotton fabric for sleeves and ruffle of classic dress
  - ½ yd (46 cm) of silky fabric for ballgown
  - Optional 3" x 32" (8 cm x 82 cm) lace edging rather than fabric ruffle for ball gown
  - Optional 1" x 14" (2.5 cm x 36 cm) lace edging for neck ruffle
  - Matching thread
  - Optional plain or metallic rickrack or braid
  - Embroidery floss for sewing rickrack or braid (optional)
  - Optional tulle, netting, or metallic mesh, and 3" (8 cm) lace edging for slip

- Crown and shoes
  - ½" (12 mm) wide gold or silver trim for crown
  - Scrap of gold or silver colored fabric for crown
  - Craft store "gems" for crown
  - Stiff felt for crown and shoe insoles
  - Felt or cotton fabric for Mary Jane shoes
  - Gold or silver fabric for princess slippers
  - Light iron-on inter facing for shoes
  - Cotton fabric for shoe lining
  - Craft foam for shoe soles
  - Snaps for Mary Jane shoes
  - Ribbon for princess slippers
  - A thin sock or ribbing knit fabric for socks
  - Tacky Glue® for shoes and crown

Equipment

- Basic sewing tools (**Tips** p. 84)
- Embroidery needles for applying optional rickrack or braid
- Air soluble pen
- Spring clothes pins for shoes

Skills

- Applying gathered lace to neck opening
- Attaching a cuff to a sleeve
- Applying rickrack or braid (optional)
- Setting in a sleeve
- Joining a gathered skirt to a dress bodice
- Applying hook and loop tape (**Tips** p. 91)

Sizes

- This pattern fits 18" (46 cm) dolls such as: Sherralyn's Dolls Kitty, dolls from the American Girl® Collection , and the Springfield® Collection.

Introduction

These instructions describe the construction of a ballgown or classic dress for eighteen inch (46 cm) dolls.

Ballgown and Classic Dress

Cutting and Marking

- If you plan to finish the neck with a lining, cut two fronts on the fold and four backs.
- If you plan to finish the neck by adding lace, cut one front on the fold and two backs.
- Cut two sleeves and two sleeve cuffs.
  - For the classic dress you may use a contrasting fabric for the sleeve.
- Cut one skirt and one skirt ruffle on the fold.
  - For classic dress you may use a contrasting fabric for the ruffle.
  - For the ballgown you may use a 3" x 32" (8 cm x 81 cm) lace instead of a ruffle.
- Mark the dots and notches.
- Mark the center front of the skirt and bodice using a pin or air soluble pen.

Finishing the Neck with a Lining

Use this method to finish the neck if you are not applying lace to the neck. If you wish to add lace to the neck skip to the section titled *Attaching Lace to the Neck.*

- Match the single notches. With right sides together, sew both sets of bodice fronts to both sets of bodice backs at shoulders. Do not finish seams.
- Press seams open.

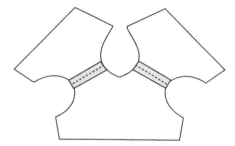

- Right sides together, pin the two bodices together at the neck.
- Sew.

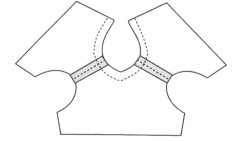

- Clip curves.

- Turn the bodice right side out and align the arm holes, sides, and bottom of bodice with the bodice lining.
- Press.
- Baste the bodice and lining together at arm holes and back opening.

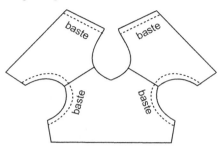

- Finish constructing the dress as if the bodice were a simple unlined bodice. Set the sleeve in the basted arm holes as if the arm hole were a single piece of cloth. Go to the section titled *Sewing a Cuff on Sleeves* to begin work on the sleeves.

Finishing the Neck with Lace

- Sewing Shoulder Seams
  - Match the single notches at the shoulder.
  - Right sides together, sew shoulder seams and finish the seams.
  - Press the finished seam to the back of the garment.

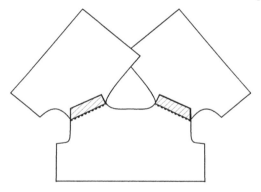

- Cut a strip of lace about 14" (36 cm) long.
- Pull a thread in the heading of the lace until it fits the neckline of the bodice. If the chosen lace does not have a heading thread, sew a gathering thread by hand or machine and pull the thread until the lace fits the neckline.

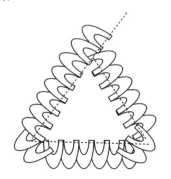

- Lay the RIGHT side of the lace on the WRONG side of the fabric. The heading edge of the lace should be next to the raw edge of the fabric at the neckline.
- Adjust the machine setting to a short zigzag. The zigzag should be the width of the lace heading.
- Zigzag the lace and fabric together.

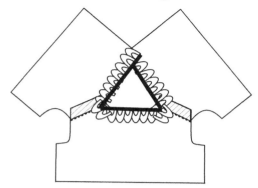

- Turn the lace to the right side of the fabric.
- The zigzagged seam should be between the lace and the bodice neckline. To hold the lace in place at the neckline, zigzag on top of the lace and over the original zigzag seam.

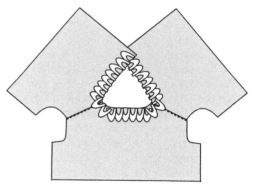

Sewing a Cuff on Sleeves

- Before sewing the cuff to the sleeve, check the fit on your doll.
  - Pin the two short sides together.
  - Try to pull the doll's hand through the cuff.
  - If the hand does not go through the cuff, cut a slightly longer cuff.
- Finish one side of the cuff.
- Sew two rows of gathering stitches at the bottom of each sleeve.

- Pull up the bottom of sleeve to fit the cuff.

- Right sides together, sew the unfinished side of the cuff to the bottom of the sleeve.

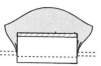

- Remove the gathering stitches.
- Fold the cuff to the inside of the sleeve as indicated on the pattern.
- Topstitch or slip-stitch the folded cuff to the sleeve.

If you wish to add rickrack or braid to the cuffs follow the direction in *Sewing Rickrack to Cuff and Waist* at the end of this section.

Setting in the Sleeves

- Gather the top of each sleeve where indicated on the pattern.

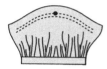

- Pull up the gathers to fit the arm hole of the bodice.
- Right sides together, pin each sleeve to the bodice. Match the dot at the top of the sleeve to the shoulder seams. Hand baste the sleeve to the bodice, if you like.
- Machine stitch each sleeve to the bodice.

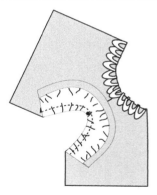

- Remove the basting and gathering stitches.
- Finish the seam.

Sewing Bodice sides

- Fold right sides of bodice together at the shoulder seams.

- Sew across the bottom of each sleeve and down the bodice's side.

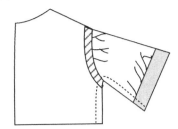

- Finish the seams.

Preparing the Skirt

- Machine or hand hem the ruffle, using a ¼" (6 mm) seam.
- Run two parallel lines of gathering stitches on the skirt ruffle. Use ¼" (6 mm) and ⅜" (9 mm) seam allowances for the two stitching lines. If your are using lace with a heading thread, you may pull the thread instead of adding machine stitches.

- Pull up the bobbin stitches until the gathered edge of the ruffle is the same length as the skirt top tier. Match the skirt center front to the ruffle center front.
- Pin the ruffle to the skirt.
- Machine stitch them together. Use the ¼" (6 mm) seam guide.

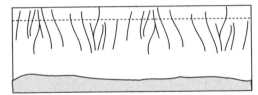

- Remove the gathering threads.
- Finish the seam.

Gathering the Skirt

- Sew two rows of gathering stitches across the top of the skirt as indicated on the pattern.

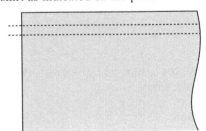

- Pull up the gathering stitches to fit the bottom of the bodice.

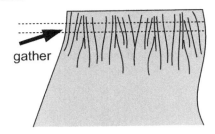

gather

Attaching the Skirt to the Bodice

- Match the center fronts and pin the skirt to the bodice. You may baste them if you like.
- Sew the skirt to the bodice.
- Remove the gathering stitches.
- Finish the seam.

Couching Rickrack or Braid to Cuff and Waist (optional)

In the couching method, the trim is applied by hand and the sewing needle will not pierce the trim.

- Use metallic rickrack or other metallic braid for the ballgown, if you wish.
- Use matching or contrasting embroidery floss to sew plain rickrack to the classic dress.
- Bring the needle to the outside of the sleeve cuff or waist line under the first rickrack peak. Pull all of the thread through the fabric.
- Insert the needle into the fabric over a rickrack valley. Pull all the the thread to the back of the fabric.
- The thread should lay across the rickrack.
- Bring the needle to the outside of the fabric under the next rickrack valley.
- Continue crossing the thread over the rickrack in the same manner.
- Never pierce the rickrack with the needle.

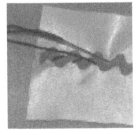

- Pull the thread all the way through the fabric each time the needle goes through the fabric.
- Secure the thread on the wrong side of the fabric.

Back Openings

I like to close this dress with a flat back seam the way the back opening would close with a zipper, rather than overlapping the back closing. This section shows how to sew the lower center back closed and leave the upper part open for hook and loop tape. If you prefer, you can apply hook and loop tape all the way down the dress back instead of sewing the lower center back closed.

- Finish each of the raw edges of the back opening. Finish the raw edges at the very end of the seam allowance, so that the total seam allowance will be available.
- Pin the back closed.
- Measure 7½" (19 cm) down from the top of the back opening and mark.
- Start at the top of the opening. Sew a ½" (12 mm) seam with a machine basting stitch. At the 7½" (19 cm) mark shorten the machine stitch length and continue sewing to the bottom of the dress.

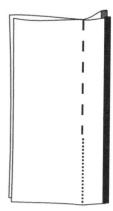

- Press the seam open and remove the basting stitches from the top 7½" (19 cm) of the seam.

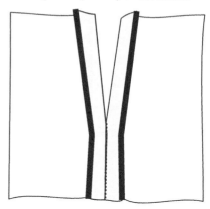

Try the garment on the doll and make any adjustments needed.
- Apply hook and loop tape. (**Tips** p. 91) Start with the third bullet point under *Closing the Back with Hook and Loop Tape*, if you have sewn the lower back closed.

Slip

For an optional slip use the classic skirt or ballgown skirt pattern and the ruffle pattern.
- Cut one skirt from tulle, netting, or metallic mesh.
- Cut a length of 3" (8 cm) lace edging using the ruffle pattern.
- Gather the lace and sew it to the bottom of the skirt.
- Fold over ¾" (2 cm) of fabric at the skirt waist.

- Sew the fabric down using an ⅜" (9 mm) seam to make a casing.
- Insert elastic into casing and pull up to fit the doll's waist.
- Sew the slip closed at the back of the slip.

Princess Crown

Preparing the Crown

- Cut out princess crown pattern from your chosen fabric.
- Glue the cut out fabric to a small piece of stiff felt.

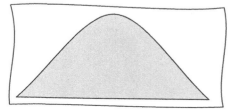

- Cut out the stiffened crown piece.
- Glue the gold or silver trim around the top of the crown piece.

- Measure around the doll's head where she will wear the crown.

- Cut a length of trim ¼" (6 mm) longer than the measurement.
- Glue the trim over the bottom edge of the crown piece. Be sure to cover the raw edges of the trim that has already been glued to the crown. The crown piece should be in the middle of the trim.

- Glue on the jewels.
- Drape the crown over a cylinder, such as the glue container, to dry. The crown will dry slightly curved and fit the doll's head more easily.

- Turn under a ⅛" (3 mm) seam allowance, and sew the ends together to make a circle.

Mary Jane Shoes and Princess Slippers

In the instructions the word "vamp" refers to the top part of the shoe or slipper.

Cutting and Marking

- Cut two vamps.
- Cut two vamp linings.
- Cut two shoe straps from matching fabric for Mary Jane shoes.
- Cut two 16" (41 cm) lengths of ribbon for princess slippers.
- Cut out two insoles from stiff felt.
- Cut out two soles from a craft foam sheet.
- Mark the dots on the vamp with air soluble pen.
- Mark the notches with air soluble pen. Do not clip notches because some of the clips would show in the finished shoes.

- Reinforce the vamps by applying iron-on interfacing to the fabric before cutting the pieces out.
- With right sides together, sew one vamp to one vamp lining all the way across the top of the vamp. Use a ¼" (6 mm) seam.
- Clip curves.

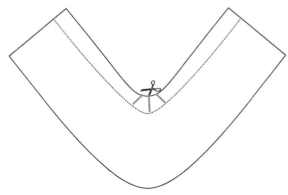

- Turn the vamp right side out so that the raw edges of the seam and the felt interfacing are hidden. Press and topstitch close to the sewn top edge all the way across the top of the vamp.
- Stay-stitch the bottom of the vamp ¼" (6 mm) from the raw edge. The fabric below the stay-stitch line will be turned under and glued to the sole.

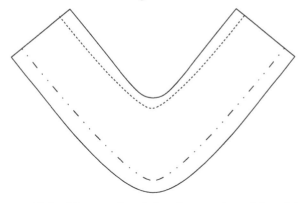

- Right sides together, bring the two short sides of the vamp together and sew.

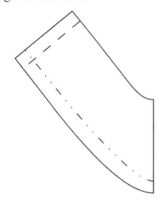

Attaching the Insole and Sole to the Vamp

- Clip the bottom of the vamp in the four places shown on the pattern. Stop each clip at the vamp's stay-stitching.

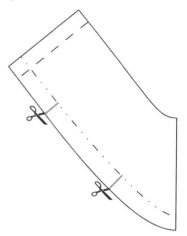

- Turn right side out.
- Hand gather the toe fabric at the bottom of the vamp until it curls around the vamp stay-stitching. The hand stitching should be very close to the cut edge. Do not secure the gathering threads.
- Insert insole into the vamp.

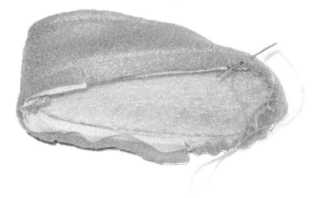

- Match the single notches.
- Match the heel seam of the vamp to the double notches.

- Hold the ungathered sides of the vamp to the insole with spring clothes pins while you work on the toe.

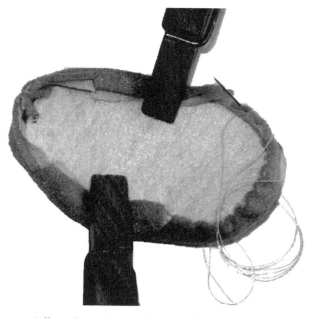

- Adjust the gathers and secure the gathering thread.
- Glue the gathered toe fabric to the insole.
- Remove the clothes pins and glue the vamp's sides to the insole from the stay-stitching to the raw edge.
- If the heel does not fit, hand gather heel fabric at the bottom of the vamp very close to the cut edge. Pull the stitches until the bottom of the heel fabric curls around the vamp's stay stitching and fits the insole.
- Glue the gathered heel fabric to the insole.

- Glue the sole to the outside of the vamp against the insole, hiding the insole and the vamp's raw edges.

- Put weights (I used pennies) inside the shoe and allow the glue to dry.

Adding Ties

- Complete both shoes before adding straps.
- Princess slippers
  - Find the midpoint of the ribbon length and hand sew it to the back seam of the slipper.
  - Put the slippers on the doll and tie.
- Mary Jane shoes
  - Fold each tie in half, right sides together.
  - Sew down one short side of the strap toward the cut edges. Pivot on the needle and sew down the length of the strap. Use an ⅛" (3 mm) seam.

  - Turn the straps right side out.
  - Use one pair of snaps for each shoe.
  - Sew one snap of each snap pair to the sewn end of a shoe strap.

  - Sew the second snap from each pair to the outside of a shoe on one of the dots marked in air soluble pen. Make a left and right shoe by sewing a snap on the left side dot of one shoe and the right side dot of the other shoe.

  - Snap a strap to each shoe.
  - Put the shoes on the doll while she is wearing socks or stockings.
  - Move the unfastened end of each strap across the doll's foot and tuck it inside the shoe where you have marked a dot.
  - Adjust the strap to fit the doll's foot and pin the strap at the dot.
  - Unsnap the shoe. Leave the strap pinned to the shoe and remove the shoe from the doll.
  - Sew the strap to the inside of the shoe by hand.
  - Sew an ornament to the toe of the shoe, if you like.

Sock

Instructions for sewing the sock are found in the sock section of the chapter titled "Pants, T-Shirt, Skirt, and Sneakers." (p. 57)

Here is Twinkle, the mini doll Kitty is holding on the cover. She is wearing the ballgown and princess crown. The patterns for Twinkle and her clothing are in this book's companion book, *Sewing for Mini Dolls*. Twinkle's patterns fit American Girl® Mini dolls and are also available at www.sherralynsdolls.com.

Ballgown and Classic Dress with Accessories

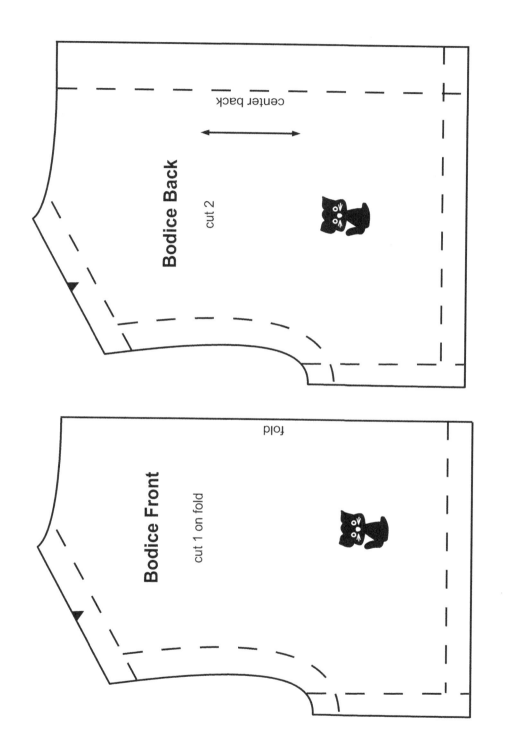

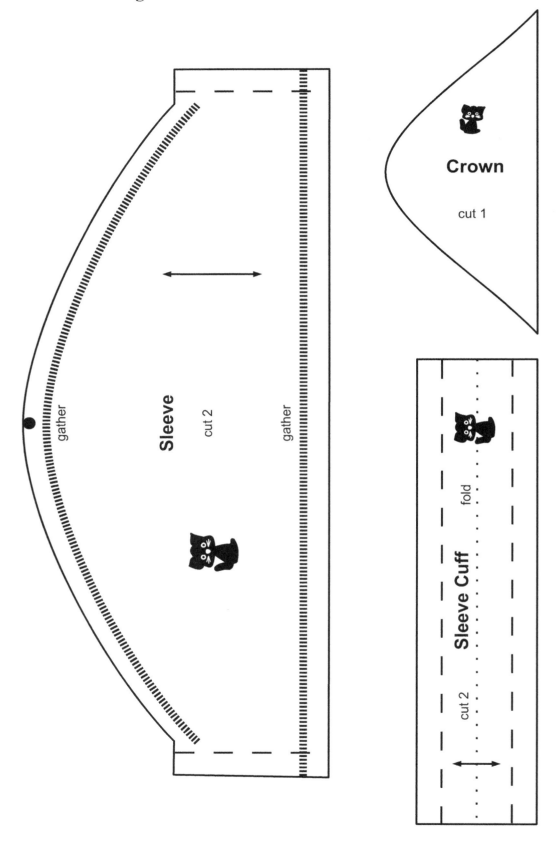

Crown

cut 1

Sleeve

cut 2

gather

gather

Sleeve Cuff

cut 2

fold

Ballgown and Classic Dress with Accessories

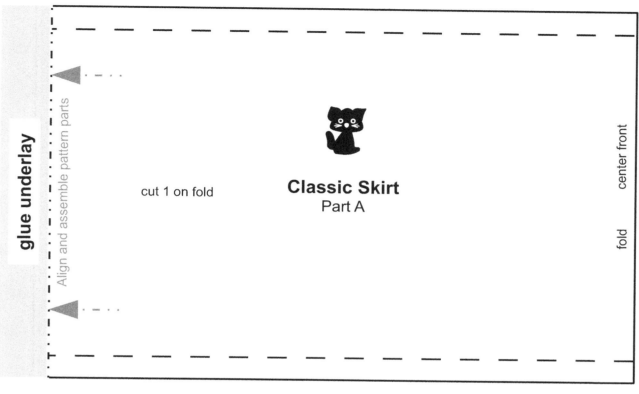

glue underlay

Align and assemble pattern parts

cut 1 on fold

Classic Skirt
Part A

center front

fold

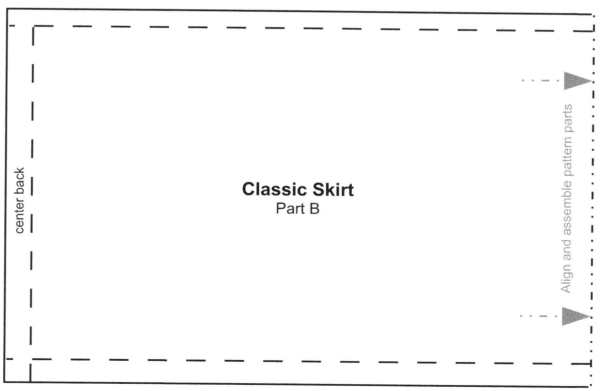

center back

Classic Skirt
Part B

Align and assemble pattern parts

Ballgown and Classic Dress with Accessories

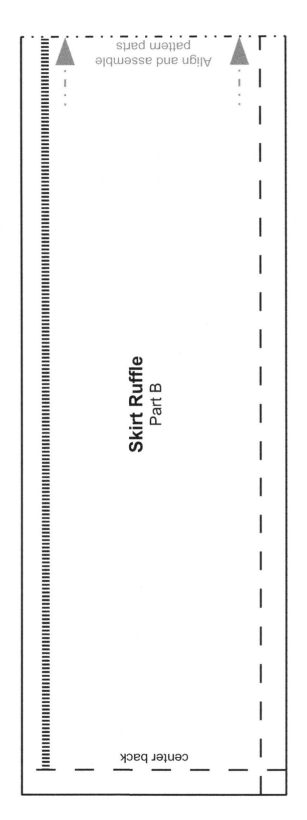

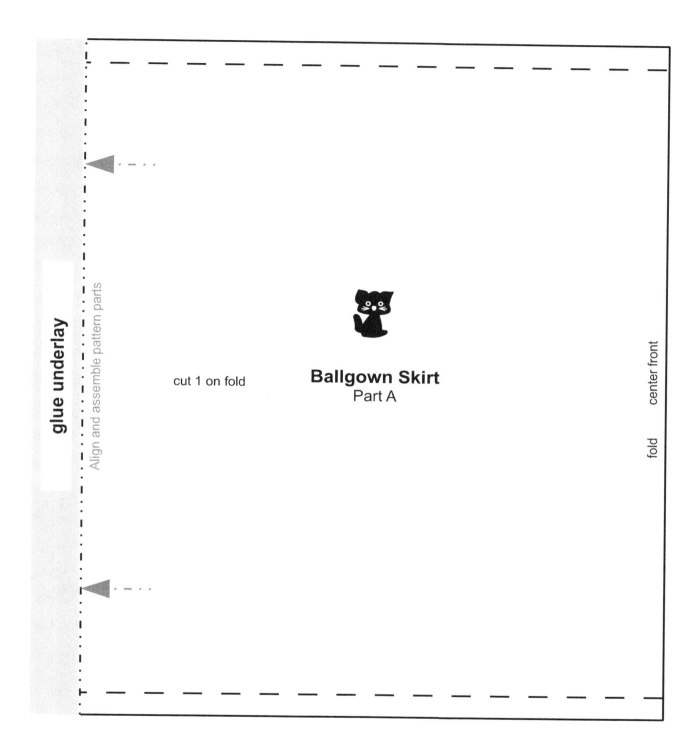

glue underlay

Align and assemble pattern parts

cut 1 on fold

Ballgown Skirt
Part A

fold   center front

Ballgown Skirt
Part B

center back

Align and assemble pattern parts

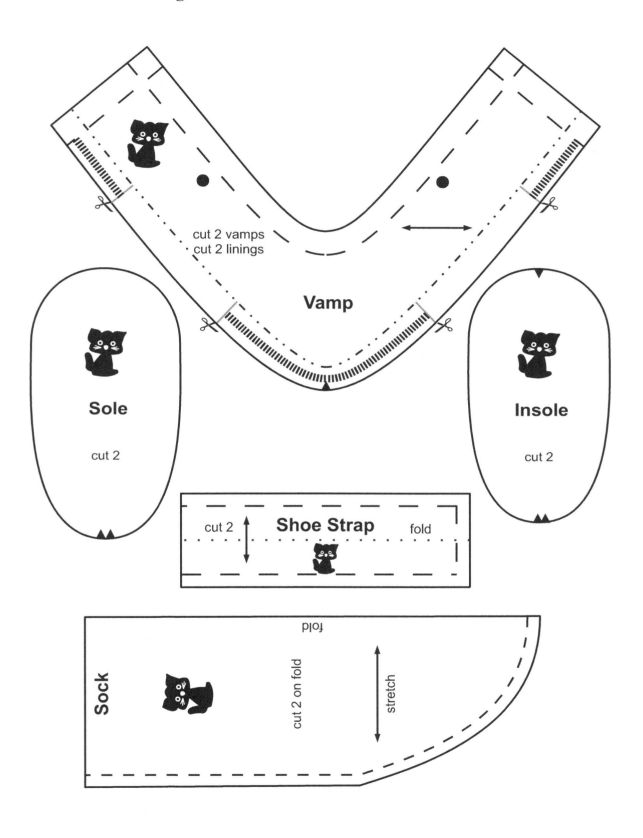

cut 2 vamps
cut 2 linings

Vamp

Sole

cut 2

Insole

cut 2

cut 2   **Shoe Strap**   fold

Sock

cut 2 on fold

fold

stretch

Tools, Tips, and Techniques

APPENDIX

The following hints have been taken from my blog and revised for the sake of continuity. Occasionally a note in my patterns will refer you to topics in this section. The topic **Basic Sewing Tools**, for example, is listed under equipment in all my patterns.

I have written other hints hoping that they might be helpful to you as you sew this doll and her clothing. Some of the short cuts that I use are not traditional methods. If you prefer traditional methods, please use them.

Sewing Machine

- It is much easier to sew doll clothes and cloth dolls if you use a sewing machine with controllable speed. A sewing machine that only has a fast speed is hard to maneuver while you are sewing short seams and small curves.
- A zigzag stitch is a must for sewing knits. Zigzagging is an easy way to finish seams on tiny doll clothes.

Basic Sewing Basket

I like sewing gadgets. I keep them in boxes and drawers all over my sewing room. If I were furnishing a sewing basket with basic sewing tools, I would list: dressmaker scissors, an assortment of pins and a pin cushion, an assortment of hand sewing needles, a thimble, and a tape measure.

- It is important that scissors are sharp and well made. I have both Gingher® and Fiskars® dressmaker shears. I can recommend either pair.

- I usually use glass head silk pins, but sometimes I use silk pins with a smaller metal head. I have an over sized tomato pin cushion and now a globe pin cushion made from the free pattern offered on my website.

- I have an assortment of hand sewing needles. Different sewing jobs need different size needles. The needle I use most often for hand sewing is a size 8 embroidery needle. For some jobs I may choose a longer or thinner needle. Occasionally I list an unusual size needle under equipment at the beginning of a pattern.
- Not everyone uses a thimble, but I can't get along without one.

- Along with my regular width tape measure I have a narrow tape measure made to use in dollmaking.

I have a few more tools that I use frequently. I have even more gadgets that I enjoy using at times. The tools that I have named are the ones that are used in most of my doll and doll clothes patterns.

Basic Ironing

It is as important to press seams between sewing steps in doll dressmaking as it is to press while making larger projects. Basic Ironing equipment is essential to sewing.
- Steam iron
- Full size ironing board
- Spray water bottle for moistening fabric if you are not using steam in your iron

More Sewing Tools

Here is a list of other sewing tools that are useful. Occasionally I list one of these tools under equipment at the beginning of a pattern.

Sewing Machine Tools

- Open embroidery foot
I use this foot when I am sewing a traced shape such as an arm or leg. The foot's openness makes the line easy to see.
- Ott-lite®
I have an Ott-lite® on my sewing table. I use it along with my open embroidery foot to stitch a traced shape.
- Patchwork foot
This foot was made for quilters, but it is great for sewing ¼" (6mm) and ⅛" (3mm) seam allowances on doll clothes.
- Zipper foot

More Sewing basket

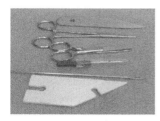

The picture shows a collection of tools that I find helpful.

- There are two different point turners in the picture.
  - The one at the top of the picture is helpful when turning curved pieces.
  - The bottom turner is helpful for defining sharp angles.

- Both turners are helpful for defining points.
- The second tool from the top is a hemostat. It is helpful for turning small fabric pieces and stuffing dolls and toys.
- I use my small scissors for clipping seams and delicate trimming.
- A seam ripper is very useful to me. I need it more often than I like to admit.
- The bodkin makes it easy to insert elastic into a casing.

More Ironing

- Doll clothes ironing board

I have a small ironing board made for pressing doll clothes that I find very useful. It makes pressing little sleeves and hems easier.

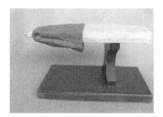

- Sleeve roll

A sleeve roll is sometimes a good choice for pressing small sewing projects, because small pieces may be pinned to it. I push the pins straight down into the roll as if it were a pin cushion.

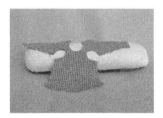

- Pressing strips

Cut ½" (12mm) wide strips from a 5" x 8" (or metric equivalent) index card printed with a ¼" (6mm) grid. To accurately press under a ½" (12mm) of fabric pull the edge of fabric over the paper strip and press. To press under ¼" (6mm) of fabric pull the fabric to the ¼" (6mm) line and press.

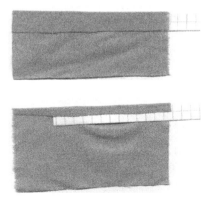

- Finger pressing

Sometimes in dollmaking the only pressing equipment that you need is a finger or two.
- To finger press a seam open spread the seam open and run your index finger or thumb down the stitch line. Put enough pressure on the stitch to encourage the seam to stay open.
- To finger press a crease in the fabric pinch the fabric between your finger and thumb at the spot where you want the crease to begin. Pull the fabric through your finger and thumb along the line to be creased. If you are not satisfied with the crease, repeat the pinch and pull process.

Stitches

Machine Stitches

- Stay stitching
  - Stay stitching is usually sewn on the stitching line of a single layer of fabric.
  - It is used to prevent fabric from stretching.
  - It is used as a guide for folding or clipping fabric.

- Topstitching
  - Topstitching will be visible on a finished garment.
  - Use the edge of the presser foot or a seam guide to produce a straight stitch.
  - Match the thread color to the fabric or choose an interesting contrast.

- Gathering stitch
  - Sew two parallel rows of long stitches and pull the bobbin threads until the fabric is gathered to the desired length.
  - Check the fabric to see if the stitches can be removed from the fabric without leaving small holes. Then one row of gathering stitches may use a ⅜" (9mm) seam guide even though the joining seam will be ¼" (6mm). Remove the visible gathering stitch after the joining seam has been sewn.
- Zigzag stitch
  - Joining knits fabric
    - Use zigzag stitches to join knit fabric.

- Use a fairly wide zigzag stitch to join knits. Set the zigzags to be fairly close together, but not a satin stitch.
- If your zigzag is not as wide as the seam allowance, you may trim the seam.

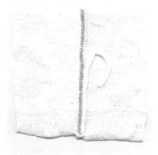

- Sewing lace to knits with the zigzag stitch
  - Lay the lace on the right side of the fabric.
  - If the lace will extend above or below the fabric, overlap the raw edge of the knit with the lace heading .

- If the lace will lie on top of the fabric make the heading even with the raw edge.
- Stitch a narrow almost satin stitch on the lace heading.

Hand Stitching

One stitch is defined as the needle going into and coming out of the fabric.
- Running stitch

Several stitches are made with the needle before the thread is pulled through the fabric.

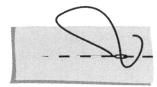

- Basting stitches

Basting stitches are running stitches used to hold fabric together so that it can be sewn with a machine stitch.
- Hand gathering

Hand gathering stitches are running stitches that are pulled so that the fabric is gathered over the thread.
- Slip-stitch
  - A slip-stitch is an almost invisible stitch. It is a good stitch to use when putting in a hem.
  - Finish the raw edge of the garment to be hemmed.
  - Press in the hem. For these patterns the hem is usually ½" (12mm).
  - Use a few pins to hold the hem in place.
  - Check the length on the doll before continuing.
  - Fold the finished edge back about ⅛" (3mm).

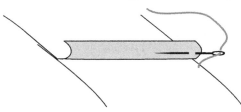

  - Take about an ⅛" (3mm) stitch through the folded back edge. Pull the thread through the fabric.
  - Catch two or three threads and take a small stitch on the part of the hem that will be visible on the dress.
  - Take the next stitch in the folded back edge. For these small hems the visible stitches should about ¼" (6mm) apart.

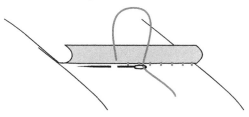

- Ladder stitch

In doll patterns and doll crafting magazines the invisible hand stitch used in doll construction is called the ladder stitch. In embroidery books the ladder stitch is a decorative stitch that looks like a ladder. The dollmaker's ladder stitch is similar to the slip-stitch, but it is done on the outside of the doll.
  - Using the ladder stitch to connect the doll's head to the body (Kitty's head is attached by machine.)
    - Insert the neck into the opening in the head.
    - Use a few pins if you like to hold the two parts together. I usually just hold the two together as I sew.
    - Take a small stitch in the head.
    - Pull the thread through each stitch as you take it.
    - Take the second stitch in the neck.
    - Go back to the head for the next stitch and make it very close to the first stitch.
    - Continue back and forth.
    - Take only one stitch at a time. Pull the thread completely through with each stitch.

- Keep the stitches very close together. You should take between fifteen and twenty stitches per inch.

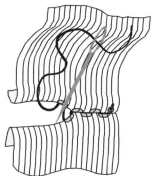

Picture courtesy Dover Publications "Easy to Make Story Book Dolls" by Sherralyn St.Clair

- Sewing arm and leg stuffing openings closed with the ladder stitch
  - Finish stuffing each piece.
  - Tuck the raw edges of the stuffing opening inside the arm or leg.
  - Hold the edges of the stuffing opening together as you sew.
  - Do not overlap the edges as you sew.
  - Take a small stitch on one side of the opening.
  - Pull the thread through each stitch as you take it.
  - Take the second stitch on the other side of the opening.
  - Go back to first side for the next stitch and make it very close to the beginning stitch.
  - Continue back and forth. Keep the stitches very close together. You should take between fifteen and twenty stitches per inch.
- Overcasting stitch
  - Using overcasting to close a body back stuffing opening
    - Start sewing at the top of the stuffing opening on the left side of the opening. Hide the thread knot by inserting the needle into the top of the stuffing opening and bringing it out on the left side.
    - Make a stitch straight across the opening to the right side.
    - Make the second stitch going right to left slightly slanted. The second stitch in each pair will be inside the closing, so that the visible stitches go straight across the stuffing opening.

- Continue back and forth keeping the outside stitching straight

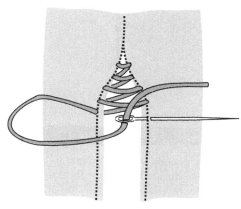

- Pull the stitches tight as you sew. The above figure shows loose stitches to illustrate thread placement.
  - Using overcasting to close an arm or leg
    - Finish stuffing each piece.
    - Tuck the raw edges of the stuffing opening inside the arm or leg.
    - Hold the edges of the stuffing opening together as you sew.
    - Sew both sides of the opening together with each stitch.
    - Keep the stitches small and close together.

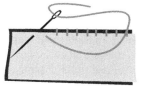

- French knot

The books I have read have different opinions on the number of times to wrap the floss around the needle while making the stitch. One book says only one wrap. One book says one or two. Another book says two or three wraps. I usually use two wraps for a French knot. To make thicker French knots, use more strands of floss.

  - Bring the needle to the right side of the fabric slightly to the right of the point marked for the French knot.
  - Pull all the floss through the fabric until it stops at the knotted end.
  - Hold the needle close to the marked point and wrap the floss around the needle twice.

○ Insert the needle through the point marked on the fabric.

Marking Fabric

First choose a pen, pencil, or other method to mark your fabric pieces. Then choose the method to use for transferring the pattern markings to the fabric. You can find other more traditional methods for marking fabric in sewing handbooks.

Choosing Pens and Pencils

- Use a thin line air soluble pen when marking on the right side of the fabric. I find that the thicker air soluble pens are not precise enough for marking small size sewing projects. Mark with this type of pen just before sewing, because it disappears quickly. Sometimes the markings will last a few hours or a few days zipped in an air tight plastic bag. The time the marking lasts depends on the age of the pen and the amount of humidity in the air.
- For marks on the wrong side of the fabric and marks for embroidery designs, I like to use Prismacolor® pencils. They wash out easily.
- If you prefer more traditional marking methods, you can purchase tailor's chalk in various colors, or try a marking wheel and transfer paper.

Tracing Markings

- Hold the pattern and fabric up to a window to trace markings. This method is easier if the pattern and fabric are held to the window with drafting tape. (I think masking tape is too strong.)
- A clear plastic box picture frame works fairly well when tracing pattern markings. It should be propped up at an angle rather than resting flat on a table. Another solution is to have a battery powered light under the plastic box. Light should be behind the pattern that you are tracing.
- My favorite tracing method is a light box or table. I bought a small inexpensive one years ago. Larger ones may be fairly pricey. I use a small amount of drafting tape to hold the pattern and fabric to my light box.

Using Freezer Paper

- If you have freezer paper, you can trace your templates onto a piece of freezer paper. Cut out the tracings and iron the waxy side of the tracing onto your fabric instead of drawing the pieces on the fabric. Use a relatively cool iron setting such as one for polyester or for cotton blends. The freezer paper method saves

time. I have been able to reuse my freezer paper tracing at least three times.

Clipping Fabric

- Cut out the small notches in the seam allowance that are used to help match fabric pieces.

- You can make a small clip in the middle of each notch if you prefer.

Cutting out Parts of a Paper Pattern

- Darts
  - Rather than tracing darts you can print out or copy a second pattern piece.
  - Cut the dart shape out of the pattern.
  - Place the pattern on the fabric piece to be marked.
  - Trace the dart where it belongs on the pattern.

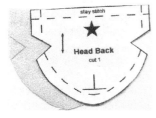

- Dots
  - Pull a pin with a small metal head through the dot on the paper pattern.
  - Put the pattern on the fabric to be marked.
  - Use a pen or pencil to mark the fabric through the hole in the pattern.

Serger

- Finishing two raw edges together
  - Sew the seam with a straight stitch on a sewing machine.

  - Serge using only three spools of thread. This method produces a narrow finished seam and a small stitch connecting the fabric pieces. Serge close to the machine stitching so that the serger knife will trim the seam to about ⅛" (3mm). Note that the bottom of the sample has not been serged to show how the serger knife has narrowed the seam.

  - Add a drop of seam sealant on the stitching at the beginning and end of each line of serging.
  - Press the seam to one side.
  - Small curves such as those on sleeves and necklines of doll clothing are difficult to do with a serger.
- Finishing single edges in hems and casings
  - Use only three thread spools to make a narrow finish.
  - Sew near the edge so that the fabric is not cut with the knife.

  - Turn up the hem the desired amount and slip-stitch.

  - For hems in A-line garments add a machine gathering stitch next to the finished edge.
  - Pull the gathering thread until the hem lies flat against the skirt and slip-stitch.

Zigzag Stitch

- Finishing two raw edges together
  - Sew the seam with a straight stitch.

  - Set the zigzag stitch about ⅛" (3mm) wide.
  - Make the zigzags close together, but not a satin stitch.
  - Zigzag close to the straight stitch so that there is about an ⅛" (3mm) raw edge.
  - Trim the seam close to the finished edge.

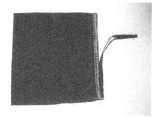

  - Press the seam to one side.

- Finishing single edges in hems and casings
  - Sew near the edge to be finished.

  - Turn up the hem the desired amount and slip-stitch.

  - For hems in A-line garments add a machine gathering stitch next to the finished edge.
  - Pull the gathering thread until the hem lies flat against the skirt and slip-stitch.

Pinking Shears

- Small curves such as those on sleeves and necklines of doll clothing are difficult to cut with pinking shears.
- Pink the seam close to the raw edge. The measurement from the peak of the pinked edge to the stitch should be almost ¼" (6mm).
- These seams may be pressed open unless they are inside an elastic casing.

- The pinked edges may be pressed in the same direction so that the machine stitching is visible inside the garment. The edges must be pressed in one direction if they will be inside an elastic casing.

Using a Seam Sealant to Finish Seams

- Lay the cut pieces that you want to treat on a sheet of wax paper.
- Squeeze a few drops of seam sealant onto the wax paper. I have tried applying the sealant directly to the fabric, but I always ended up with too much on the edges. Too much sealant makes the fabric edges stiff and difficult to sew through.
- Use a toothpick to apply a small amount to the outside edges of the fabric pieces.
- To make the sealed edges softer, after the sealant has dried, soak the treated pieces in a bowl of water. After five or ten minutes remove the fabric from the water. Blot the pieces and let air dry. Press. The fabric is soft and easy to sew. This soaking step is optional.
- These seams may be pressed open unless they are inside an elastic casing.

Casings

- To insert elastic into doll clothes casings I always use ⅛" (3mm) elastic and my favorite bodkin.

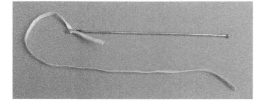

- Use your whole length of elastic. Do not cut it until it is secure on both sides of the casing. Use a bodkin to pull the elastic through the casing.
- If a seam is inside the casing, the two seam edges should have been finished together and pressed to one side. The bodkin should travel over the stitching first and then over the two seams.

- Pull the elastic through the casing with the bodkin.
- Release the elastic from the bodkin and secure the released end to the casing by sewing through it several times.

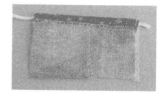

- Check the pattern instructions for measurement. Gather the casing fabric over the elastic to the desired length without stretching the elastic.
- Try the garment on to check the size.
- Secure the second side of the elastic to the second casing opening by sewing through it and the casing several times.

- Cut off the excess elastic.

Closures

Closing the Back With Hook and Loop Tape

I like to close garments for dolls with short pieces of hook and loop tape. In this method the left and right sides of the closing will be side by side like a zipper closing rather than overlapping like closings with buttons or snaps. I do not use the overlap method for hook and loop tape in these patterns, because the overlapped closing is too thick on such small dresses.

- Use your favorite method to finish each side of the opening.
- Press each finished side of the opening ½" (12mm) to the inside.
- Take a 1" (2.5cm) length of ¾" (18mm) wide hook and loop tape. The hook side and the loop side of the tape should be fastened.
- Split this tape in half lengthwise so that there are two 1" (2.5cm) lengths of ⅜" (9mm) tape.

- Separate the tape into the hook and loop sides.

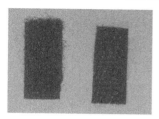

- Take the hook side of one of the tape pairs and lay it face up partly under the right side of the opening at the top of the opening. About ¼" (6mm) of tape should stick out of the opening and about ⅛" (3mm) of the tape should be under the fabric edge of the opening. The bumpy hook side of the tape should be touching the fabric at this ⅛" (3mm) overlap.
- At the edge of the right back opening stitch through the fabric and the tape.
- Lay the first piece of loop tape completely inside the left side of the back opening. The loops should be out and the smooth side of the tape should be against the fabric.
- Stitch down the tape through the fabric.
- At ⅛" (3mm) from the bottom of the tape, pivot on the needle and stitch a few horizontal stitches.
- Pivot on the needle again and stitch back up the tape.

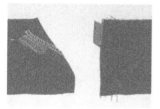

- For garments that need a second strip of hook and loop tape measure ½" (12mm) down from the first piece of loop tape and sew the second piece of tape in the same manner as the first tape.

- I like to use snag free Velcro®. The snag free variety sticks to itself, so you don't need to worry about hook and loop sides. To use this type of tape, split a single 1" (2.5cm) length of tape in half lengthwise so that you have two narrow 1" (2.5cm) lengths. Use one piece in place of the hook side and one piece in place of the loop side in the above instructions.

Closing the Back with Snaps

If you prefer an overlapped closing, use small snaps.
- Press under ½" (12mm) at back left closing and ¼" (6mm) at back right closing.

- Overlap right over left ¼" (6mm).
- Check fit on doll before applying snaps.
- Use two to four snaps to close dress.

Other Books by Sherralyn St. Clair

Sewing for Mini Dolls - Full size patterns for 6½" mini doll outfits

This book is a collection of patterns for mini dolls (6½" or 16.5 cm). The book includes full size patterns and detailed sewing instructions for the Twinkle cloth doll and her outfits. In addition to Sherralyn's Dolls Twinkle, the outfits will fit American Girl® Mini and other mini dolls. Measurements are given in both US and metric units.

The patterns include: Nightgown, Smock Top, and Two Tiered Skirt; A-line Dress, Jacket, and Bloomers; Pants, Shorts, Skirt, and T-shirt; Ballgown and Classic Dress; Shoes, Slippers, Sandals, Sneakers, and Boots; as well as Twinkle Cloth Mini Doll, Camisole, and Panties. Most of these patterns match those found in this book, *Sewing for Large Dolls*

Sherralyn's Tools, Tips, and Techniques is included.

Learn to Sew for Your Doll - A Beginner's Guide to Sewing for an 18" Doll

If you would like to teach a special child how to sew, this book presents a series of skills in a learning sequence that takes the new seamstress from the first use of a sewing machine through making an attractive wardrobe for a doll. The book gives the student a place to start and then builds on the initial skills.

This book includes instructions and full size patterns for 18" doll clothes. Measurements are given in both US and metric units.

Skills taught include: pattern reading and cutting, machine stitching, finishing seams, gathering, sewing casings, topstitching, hemming, and attaching closures.

Sew a Small Doll and Her Clothing - Full size patterns for 7½" Florabunda and her outfits

This book is a collection of patterns for the small Florabunda dolls (7.5" or 19 cm). The book includes full size patterns and detailed sewing instructions for the Florabunda cloth doll and her outfits. In addition to Sherralyn's Dolls' Florabunda, the outfits will fit Madam Alexander®'s Wendy, Vogue®'s, Modern and Vintage Ginny, as well as Lillian Vernon®'s doll.

The patterns include: Nightgown, Smock Top, and Two Tiered Skirt; A-line Dress, Jacket, and Bloomers; Pants, Shorts, Skirt, and T-shirt; Ballgown and Classic Dress; Shoes, Slippers, Sandals, Sneakers, and Boots; as well as Florabunda Cloth Doll, Camisole, and Panties. These patterns match those found in the book, *Sewing for Mini Dolls*

Sherralyn's Tools, Tips, and Techniques is included.

Easy-to-Make Storybook Dolls - A "Novel" Approach to Cloth Dollmaking

This unique guide to making 14" cloth dolls offers patterns for the eternal op ®timist, Pollyanna, as well as Dorothy from *The Wonderful Wizard of Oz* and Mary of *The Secret Garden*. Perfect for beginners, this manual will also appeal to more experienced dollmakers.

All three characters use the same basic doll body and accessories such as hats, shoes, and slips. Dorothy's wardrobe, based on descriptions of her clothing in Oz books, comprises six dresses and a nightgown. Mary's ensemble includes five dresses, a coat, and a housecoat; and Pollyanna's costumes consist of six dresses and a gown. Extras include Dorothy's green spectacles and Toto the terrier; a bed cover, and a pillow for Mary; and Pollyanna's pets, Fluffy the cat and Buffy the dog.

Sherralyn's Dolls

Visit my web site at www.sherralynsdolls.com to get more fun out of your pattern books. Here's some of what you can find there.

Patterns

The Patterns page contains patterns for doll clothes, accessories, and cloth dolls of various sizes. Many of the patterns in my books can be purchased separately for download from this web page.

You can also find a free sundress pattern for three sizes of small dolls, a free sewing tips booklet, and free miniature quilt block patterns.

Florabunda's Page

This page is kid friendly with a music video and fun surprises.

It has free sewing and craft projects that let kids make accessories for themselves and their dolls.

My free stories can inspire kids to use their dolls for creative play.

My Books

On My Books page you can find color versions of outfits from the books. E-mail me whenever you have sewing questions.

Blog

Check my blog page for sewing hints and thoughts on sewing. Feel free to leave a comment and start a discussion.

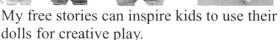

Made in United States
North Haven, CT
29 November 2021

11719706R00052